Please, Don't Go

The Conspicuous & the Dystopian Revelations

Lyle Light

*"Praying with the Rosary is the greatest
weapon against the underworld."*

– Lyle

"I asked God to whom I am, he said "Guardian of Truth" Representing the pursuit of knowledge and critical thinking to discern truth.

Pushing someone to be better is not an attack, but an attack to love.

Helping someone when knowing they can't help you back is simply a part of the human experiences. People are easier to act negative, but act cowardly afraid to open the heart. Perceive me as a Prophet Philosopher if you must so.

Philosophers use their love of knowledge to ponder questions that don't necessarily have answers. Through close reading, logical analysis and experimental thought, philosophers look to develop a deeper understanding of our universe and provoke meaningful conversations about the human condition. According to most historical accounts, Socrates is considered the "father of philosophy" as he is credited with founding Western philosophy through his unique method of questioning and critical thinking, known as the Socratic method. I wondered if I reincarnated from one of the deity's of our pasts we learn from.

Prophets: A prophet is a person who speaks for God, conveying God's message and will to others about – Responsibilities, Correcting Moral, Religious abuses, Proclaiming Moral, Religious Truths, Guiding the States, and Checking attempts at Illegality and Tyranny. As maybe, I could be both.

As I asked above, being the Guardian of Truth & Transparency of a Prophet Philosopher.

"The Bible refers to gold a lot when referring to Heaven. Gold is also referenced when a person is being refined. Positive: Dreaming/Visions of the color gold could represent that one has completed a certain process of refinement. It could also indicate a heavenly presence or a gift from God. Such as the spiritual gift of healing."

Tommy Lyle Robinson II

Owner of this book

"Please Don't Go" teaches us that everything is in your mind, whether it's true, false, dark, or funny. Your mind is the world you create that you can control. In reality, you can't really control the world. Whereas within your mind, you can create your world with motivation, dedication, failure, lessons & wisdom. Or you can sit back and let the world ride you. The 555 rule I follow within my path & mindfulness of being just aware... 5 Temples of Life to follow- Mind, Body, Soul, Spirit & Ancestry. 5 Momentums to follow along your journey- Peace, Love, Forgiveness, Awareness & Control. 5 Sights to Survive Relationships- Morals, Respect, Loyalty, Communication & Personality. If you can put these rules within your mind, then staying out of the dark is what I am supposed to teach us. As I hope it worked.

Contents

Introduction..1

A Message to Readers...2

Chapter 1: Part 1- Gathering Your Attention...........................23

Chapter 1: Part 2- The Beginning 26

Chapter 2: Drop Out Adventures 37

Chapter 3: New Ideas & New Scenery 49

Chapter 4: New Start, New Sight................................67

Chapter 5: The Teachings 82

Chapter 6: My Other Thoughts 98

Chapter 7: What Happened to Me...........................108

Chapter 8: Aug 28th...118

Chapter 9: Recap and Reiki 125

Chapter 10: Back In NY 133

Chapter 11: Getting Evidence 147

Introduction

A possibly true story that explains the path of my unknowledgeable belief on how the world works. I have made mistakes, but I also found time, thought & consideration; if we are still able to "Think," we can also "Act" & go back to fix what you or I have broken. I became ordained & learned Reiki due to an unwelcomed phenomenon by a so-called local unhinged woman and friends with bad intentions. Behold, things are hidden from us & some are far worse than what I would not do to my neighbor but only supply Law. I may have answers to fix our issues. For what information did I gather from Spirit?

Could this vaguely describe a New Prophet? Though we are told to stay away from those "types of people," but why? Those who want to prove promising ideas tend not to go far. The system wants you to believe you do not have a purpose. You are only here to work. In the meantime? Figure yourself out in between. I took time off to do it. Regardless of whether you can afford it, try to live with the basic things, as I did. We all have light. If you read this story, you might find that you can author your own novel, too! Please follow along for more. We only have one lifetime. What if I can help change yours?

If one voice is enough

Who.

Will.

Listen

A Message to Readers

"All truths hidden, become infectious."

- Lyle

This book is for you to gather insights on certain areas that may feel like they're not explained.

I want you, the reader, to inherit the differentials of any thought-provoking or open-ended narratives, to gather the intellectual information given, and to inspire your thought on what could happen next in something that may confuse you. I want to confuse you. I want us to use our own brains to have you think, "Why?" Could it be that I am sharing too much truth? That certain areas needed and not explained well could be to save the character?

Certain areas may feel unevenly paced or tightly impactful. Remember, this is a story about a character trying to remember everything within their life, from birth to teen-hood, adulthood, after going through deep conflicts between their mistakes and others.

If you feel lost, then that's the first start. A start to use your imagination.

"To understand what's going on in our land of life, you need to unlearn everything that has been taught to fully grasp the perceptions of untold truths, you'll find at your own accord."

- Lyle

To those who understand, it's about vague dynamics on how to preserve information. My idea of true vs. false remains in the air for you, the reader, to concept it.

- Lyle

"Also, remember, I am not of any affiliated religion, just following my heart. As I see the destruction of others within religion. Why must one be of hate? When you can love one another or go about your own day. Without chaos. So call me a Christian, or any other faith, as none are set in stone for me. Why did God let me see and express what I wrote for you? If I had to be baptized? Or sit in Church every Sunday. Praise him, but not always. Praise your family."

– Lyle

The 5 Negative Traits to Learn, But Not Follow

This is what the Dark Forces try to agendize for your body's temple.

5 Negative Traits

1. Anger slays Wisdom

2. Fear slays Dreams

3. Jealousy slays Trust

4. Drama slays Respect

5. Laziness slays Ambition

Now read that in reverse.

Reader:

This statement is in the front of the book, because I want you to read it, get the idea, then, I want to further the concept of our reality lie with you within the book, if you get confused. Use this as a little reference reminder.

I consider this Evidence of our Time, to wake us UP. Science says, earth is millions years old, but why does our internet say different? An AI system of Knowledge... created by Man. Could it be not so false? Or who's telling the truth? People who believe in the higher power that spread correct ideals, should understand my point. Or the not so believers that ruin concepts for others to brainwash you and laugh at you within the science realm, keep laughing. I'll laugh at you, with you... When it's actually, God who's the real scientist. Those who understand Religion, it's about actions, as Science, is about outcomes. Guess what? They equal themselves out. If humans are from another planet. Then this is my equation-

Living Species + Universe + Science ÷ by Energy = God our Creator.

Again, science says- That the Earth is millions of years old... Humans to be around 300,000+ years old. Yet a high tech development AI system, says otherwise, to slowly speak facts as the lies are being washed away slowly with truth in front of OUR faces. The pictures posted, isn't what made me " think " we founded this earth 2,024 years ago, but I found out, by seeing what isn't being told to us. I mention the James Webb Telescope, later in the book. As Andromeda Galaxy, is the closest Star Galaxy that we came from. I want to explain this to you, to hopefully gain the mobility to make changes on what you think is real, along with trying to make us better. They also say according to the Bible Earth is 4,000-6,000 years old. As it rebirthed itself from a previous nuclear impact around that time. It healed itself & turned into the beautiful Garden of Eden as differently mentioned in the Bible. Due to metaphors, that some pick up, to those who don't.

4

We came back to this place, thinking they destroyed the evil that pre-existed. I express more further in the reading, so when you read it, you'll remember this.

It's okay, I guess science is 100% right. People like me get put down, like we're the problem/crazy one. Yet when that happens? The crazy person turns out right. When lies are made from excuses to equal a truth.

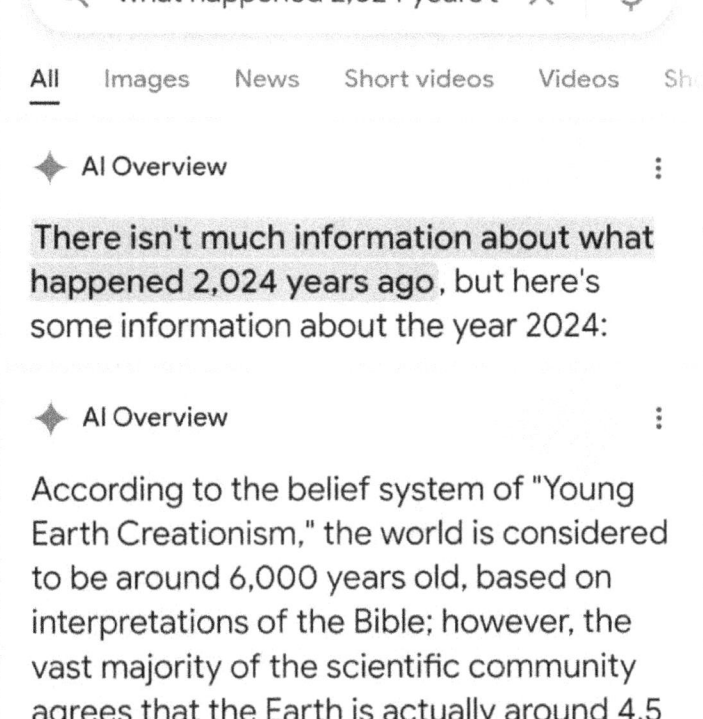

Not all conspiracies are true, but when things don't add up, to what you add up yourself? Then... We have a problem on our hands due to lack of people not fighting for our existence & untold past. I see our past vividly, to the destruction of our own future. What's meant to happen. Will happen.

Don't let our "Owners" scare us into something that will eventually make you succumb to your own weakness. Or just be lazy, & allow them to do so, with NO action. Yet WE THE PEOPLE wonder why we can't make changes. Look at the 2 pictures, really read them & look, to hope you start consuming what I say, to understand it. I've talked to superiors, who haven't denied this claim. So why not follow through with it? God let's you see, if you ask & are patient. It comes in the form of Frequency Knowledge Transfers from the higher power. Also, you think God will give a corrupt King scriptures to enact his own false teachings to submit a new agenda in the Kings Bible? Being in a Royal spot? Most of your real Prophets are shut out. As the fake play the game & steal our money for greed. As the current Royal & past families have been caught abusing tax payer funded money.

"If an official goes after the civilians, that look through finances, but we can't see the finances of our Tax money? That's the first sign of bureaucrats. Indeed it is."

- Lyle

"WE tend to suffer on Imagination then in Reality. There's a difference, when you foresee the untold to note, you can't do much about it sometimes then to "Wish" about it."

- Lyle

The only one that was for the people was Princess Diana. The others, didn't know how to show compassion. Yet they proclaim to have power. Power to steal, that's about it & a protected family name written in stone, so their family stays rich from a thief created system. Using & abusing Religion with the Pope for there own Prosperity. Our King, is just a President with

6

a term limit. Imagine that. Speaking of greed- As I do speak more of it within the book. I want to note, I foresee a lot of conflicts with Health Insurances as well. Due to Ceo's taking in millions from damaged patients. They need to merge businesses together, with merged benefits, as they can put their income/money in one big account. No need for several separate insurance companies. Variety is great, but Variety Programs in the Health Dept., kills people. Shouldn't we revaluate importance? They're business model? Is to deny as many claims to off set the purchases given. Then, they'll give you an excuse why they're greedy, to off set their millions.

If someone says that can't be done? They don't want to have things easier for you. That's all, because they know they won't make millions on sick people's insurance.

Take THAT into consideration.

"For those that ask, why? Is our current understanding a lie? Perhaps, or could it be that the Vatican is filled with centuries of teachings that are withheld. Only certain ones out of a 53-mile archive were chosen to be put in the Bible. What gives them the right to hide information from us? We THE PEOPLE should own this, as they should all be uploaded to a huge Archive Data research center.

"If some God's are of many years of age from the scriptures, it's because of the age system of each traveled Realm in Space, as to Earths rotation of every 24hrs, as others are more or less throughout space age relativity that affects human age."

– Lyle

Why did I write this? How does this conflict affect my life?

How can I relate my troubles or character and express how I am in pain to others? How can I learn from my mistakes and from the atrocious acts that others have inflicted upon me?

In my life, I have made some mistakes, but I don't always stay negative anymore. No matter what your indulgences are, know that God and the Higher power will forgive you. As long as you forgive yourself, you can rest assured with the hope that many others will also understand you.

Faith led me to write this book. I received my SIGN the night of Jan 27th, then within seven days, Feb 3rd, when I got up to 35,000 words with only two days to revise. Then, between that time, I worked on the final product and what you are currently reading. I am not a writer nor much of a reader, but I have put my all into the book so that I can tell my story and inspire others.

The path you should follow will hit you at the moment you least expect it! Why would I write this? You can blame me or say that I am using my fantasy mind and making up things. If only that was the case here. Well, guess what? It isn't. I mean, I have been bullied for who I am as a person, and people randomly tell me, "No one likes you," for no reason, to just hurt me. I have been drugged and then laughed at. I could have done major damage to the people that hurt me, but why would I do that? All I want to do is bring attention to what they have done to me. If you have been in a situation like mine, write about it!

"We live in a World, where the intelligent must be silent, so the unintelligent don't get offended."

– Author

I have also noticed things out of this realm; we are not alone. We have realms for a reason. Seven, to be exact, to represent each Chakra within our given Temple by our Lords. Similar to the Native American ideals of the 7 sisters of The Pleiades. As Earth is an 8th Realm which is Helis. I want you to grasp the fact that no one is perfect in this Earth realm. Being on Earth is almost on par with being in being the legit hell. Hell isn't a real place. It is a fictional place used to scare you. Suppose you do NOT forgive or do not have goodness in your own heart; you most likely will be tossed in Purgatory. There, you will do slave work for the realms. This is the slave earth. You RENT your land and the house you 'own.' You don't really own it. So yes, this is the Purgatory realm; it is for us to learn before we can ascend to our true selves.

I also wrote this because we need a better understanding of how the world actually works. For example, Death is a part of life, right? So, when someone dies, essentially, past lives' mistakes (Karma) come into play in how you die. We have feelings brought on to us by our maker. So, we have to deal with Yin and Yang. Get the point yet? We will cry when a loved one dies. It may seem like it was too soon, or it shouldn't have happened at all. We also need to remember what happens in other realms does ripple back to us. Can you be mindful of the cycle you're stuck in? Break it with the power of Grace.

My mistakes, others' mistakes and the conflicts in between have let the higher power show me a Golden S, which I'll talk more about in the book. I think I was Saved. Why else would I see a vision of a Golden S? If others have seen it, should we all get together? Start a better cause than just being human. Have morals and respect. Doing things for just yourself is great, but remember, you didn't get here just by being lucky, a gift from above has brought you and me into this world FOR A REASON. One of my reasons is in your hands...

Why is it so hard for us to just be decent? I think about us when I should think about me. I am a Taurus. Earth is my sign! So, when I feel trouble on our lands, I have the BALLS to speak up and call out what needs to be done, OR at least I try.

Suppose I were to ever run for any office; guess what? The opponent can't use my mistakes against me when I wrote this book. Why is it that every person running has to be dirty to one another? Why can't we just run based on knowledge, common sense, and likability? If the person hasn't greatly affected communities in a bad way but is just themselves, then what does it matter? There is no need to bring up the things they did before office.

I am hoping to get us back on track to a better tomorrow to bring Wisdom to you.

They say one voice is enough.

Will mine be enough for you? To help SAVE you?

:/ -Says Spirit to Lyle.

Why is the Pope mentioned in the book?

I talk about the Pope. When you read and gather the information I put within, you will understand more.

Those who understand Religion should note and comprehend that back in the day, the Catholic royals took scriptures from Christian royals; that's why they battled, and nobody knows the true meaning of what God intended, as I may know some. God is ALL knowing. With scriptures taken, note, we follow something stolen. Wouldn't that be the first clue something could be off?

The Pope is a fictional member of society. Back then, they needed someone to play a role, and now, it has been played for the past 266 of them. Why is it that when a woman or male priests have relations in a way that is unnatural and harmful, they label them GAY or Homosexual? WHY not a Pedophile? Why does the GAY community need to receive backlash? All of this comes from an unjust EMPIRE of people pretending they are doing the right thing but are also stirring an Agenda to demonize our way of life. Control-ism! and Brainwashing.

Plus, hasn't the Pope already been caught bad-mouthing the LGBTQ community and then apologized for it? Then, he did it again, not too long after the first time.

"To those of differences in how you feel within of opposite sex of what you were born, of those wanting to participate in Sports, as it's a gift for Sports not a right.

You should start a Union Sport, that indulges on all sports, but teams are of different sex & same, like a Olympics, but for Trans Athletes. Don't push to be apart of a concept that was created to separate the different strengths between sexes, prior to those wanting to get beat by the same or opposite sex to establish such sport to indulge on that. It's not fair if a Woman gets beat by a Trans Woman who was once a male & Vise Versa. Wouldn't that mean? You are pushing to be unfair? Then complain about others not being fair to your cause? As I'm a Gay Independent. With basic understanding of human equalization. Not separation. There's a BIG difference..."

- Author

"Show love and mind your business."

– Bob Marley

"Diversity is a GREAT THING. But when it comes to critical & dangerous jobs? Diversity should be last on the list, as knowledge and priority of the job needed to be done at a successful rate is essentially more beneficial. Then putting someone in a position that has no clue or no effort to go beyond ones mind. Unless that person of diverse backgrounds has the ability to do the job. As I think we're losing common sense. Because we want to include diversity in everything. Again, be sure all has the knowledge rather than putting someone in a position that doesn't understand and has failures or results of death. We're smarter than this."

– Author

"Instead of Pride Day? Let's take Martin Luther King Jr.'s day, which he marched for Humanity? Why can't we just make that Humanity's Day for all? Instead of subjecting ourselves into separate groups, separating our minds, rejoining and stop labeling yourselves to start the line of judgment against character that you inflict on others if someone doesn't like your view, instead of actions. A CHARACTER is someone who dresses up half naked for a pride event in tight high shorts, shirt above the belly. As children are around. I'm a Gay Independent here with Morals. Shine the Pride flag high, but don't ridicule someone who doesn't like it and yell at them. That's a bad ACTION. Be nice. Same with bigots. Stay in your lane, and the LGBTQ should stay in theirs. Just a thought…"

-Author

"Christians don't judge on Orientation, to judge of 2 peoples love, is the hate of Devil not the heart of the Lord. As it coordinated by people who hated it. If God hated it? Why say Love for all? As it's a contradicting statement coerced for us to not understand it, if you hate on love, you perish with Satan, as it will be."

– You're Guardian of Truth-

"Catholic Royals judged orientation as Christian Royals picked up and aligned what the Pope (Catholic) gave to a Christian. Then now we have judgement against orientation due to those 2 conducting change for an Agenda as what was rewritten/deciphered, as there is NO said real scriptures from Jesus, only notes from others to novels as such an align you with thus idea of separation. Why did he give me a Golden S? As only heaven has gold. I shall help this matter, listen to me now. All is equal under love. Those who hurt others physically, or on purpose with no reason, shall be done by thus reverse & law.

- Prophet Philosopher Lyle Light (Tommy)

- Guardian of Truth –

"To those of differences in how you feel within of opposite sex of what you were born, of those wanting to participate in Sports, as it's a gift for Sports not a right.

You should start a Union Sport, that indulges on all sports, but teams are of different sex & same, like a Olympics, but for Trans Athletes. Don't push to be apart of a concept that been created to separate the different strengths between sexes, prior to those wanting to get beat by the same or opposite sex to establish such sport to indulge on that. It's not fair if a Woman gets beat by a Trans Woman who was once a male & Vise Versa. Wouldn't that mean? You are pushing to be unfair? But complain about others not being fair to your cause? As I'm a Gay Independent. With basic understanding of human equalization. Not separation. Big difference..."

- Lyle

"Men have men sports, woman have woman sports. Trans? Can most definitely have Trans sports, that doesn't reflect on the uncomfortableness upon a male or female of none Trans Athletes. Create your own. They did. Why can't you? It's not being unfair. It's called fair on all spectrums believe it or not. Again, judging straights that are uncomfortable, is the same feeling of you judging them for not wanting to participate with none different sexes, due to strengths."

Lyle (A gay Independent by the way)

How is it that God tells you to love one another and not judge, but we do it anyway? We hate each other and say negative things about ourselves or our enemy. When an argument happens, doesn't it end up with BOTH sides apologizing in the end?

13

We need to wake up and start smelling the BS around us before it's too late.

I am not bad-mouthing a Religion, but only spewing truth if you let your mind see it.

Should the Pope start understanding me? Or our true selves? Or should the ones not supportive of others spew an agenda of hate and dis-likeness be canceled?

Or are we going to pretend all of this is okay?

If you don't understand this book, then there IS no help for you until you do.

Amen.

PS.

Tell me something that is not in the Bible. What do people think it is?

The answer: White people.

So how could God be a White person?

They didn't exist at that time. Primarily, it was Jews and some light-skinned people from the European region who were there during the times of the Bible. Even around the time he devoted his teachings within the region, nobody was of white color.

This is because skin color was not a way to categorize nations or tribes in the ancient world. So, why do we?

Lyle

Put an end to it. Now. Focus on behaviors, not color.

People with psychosis typically experience delusions (false beliefs, for example, that people on television are sending them special messages or that others are trying to hurt them) and hallucinations (seeing or hearing things that others do not, such as hearing voices telling them to do something or criticizing them). Our own system analyzes people who believe they are receiving signs from God and labels them as crazy. Yes, people with bipolar disorder and schizophrenia/delusional disorders need special care. That care is expensive because the system profits from the "insane" by keeping them institutionalized if their insurance covers it. They will take every penny until they can't anymore.

The medication to make these individuals civilized can cost patients between $15,000 and $40,000. So, you can't become better unless you give them money, or you might die. Even though they have created a solution, it doesn't mean all people will benefit. Maybe we should set up a program to help lower costs and then establish small payment arrangements to meet the needs of both parties. But no, it's always about what the state wants, not you!

We could just help each other. How long would that actually take? Without people having to explain it to us and then motivate us to act? We should have had this motivation from the beginning. If every single business or person with extra funds got together, we could help with a lot of things. I'll explain more as we journey through this horizon of storms and sunshine.

Before I do, the next couple of pages will explain more about this project.

God wants us to know and be aware that purgatory is a "pre" term context. Mostly, the system is putting the criminals in jail and prison, but some get put in the psych ward. Our government brings you a Bible in jail/prison to make you closer to God. This is good, but here's the catch! Those who "contact" God or say they have had a conversation with Him or found their purpose are labeled as "crazy," or they say they have some type of "behavioral issue."

I foresee. The best defense that we may already have or will have under our belt is a heat wave laser that is from space to take out the enemy quicker than they can blink. Similar to a Navy ship heat laser. Imagine that. Don't believe me or believe me. We live in a world where the unexpected will happen with the little things you didn't expect that seem from out of this world.

"If the Leader of the Federal Gov't takes away Federal workers none discrimination in the Federal workplace, is solely to fire a corrupt entity at a quicker rate than, to go by paperwork protocol of evidence so they can hide something between the time of findings to outcome. Stopping corruption is to stop giving it a bone to chew before they need a new bone."

– Lyle

"George Soros & Klaus Schwab – who are the acting "Satan" among other elites who are servants to the evil that's alive or to those futuristic ideas against the people. That agrees with WEF agenda. Their agenda is one that "from its heart hates Christian Europe's traditions and civilization." Starting or conditioning a Great Reset by Klaus, the founder of World Economic Forum. That tells countries what to do, or try's to do so. Is our President not of high power? When someone who starts WEF? Is the boss? Cause he has money and wants to shape the world into his fate. We THE PEOPLE are not allowing this. Not 2 rich men and others hidden of Devil minded deals." They're the next crime against humanity, well trying to be."

– Author

"If an official goes after the civilians, that look through finances, but we can't see the finances of our Tax money? That's the first sign of bureaucrats. Indeed it is."

– Author

If I were a President or shown a President, how to handle Illegal Criminals to murderers of our own. This is what I would say to offer-

"To the people of the United Equals Country & States of all ethnicities and diverse backgrounds that cover this nation as a Whole United function system & Abroad societies to what we create, learn & prosper from each other's values.

As your President, a guider protection to our roots & structures, admit full authority to offer solutions to our none, United enemies, by strengthening our Numbers & Wars, if any are to be. That we offer any Criminal Immigrants to criminals arrested, & our current prisoners of our own, at home of serious offensives, can stay in line, or accept a debt free, and quicker response of freedom, if wanting to be listed in the military, to establish a great bond between you're people, our people, and abroad to note, we are a family of immigrants, but in this ERA of time, we have terror galore, in the mix of the difficult decisions needed as leaders face, if a Nation can't sustain transparency, compatabilism of Nature's and Morals, to sustain a living Society for all, not for some. Shall be of no service & shall not call our nation, or any land thereof around us, or afar will call this earth their home if murder upon 1 or many is within your ideals.

We must defeat all enemies of evil, foreign and domestic that intend on violence thereof.

As people with hearts, choosing to hate isn't a law, but it's a must as years go by, and I hope division's way out.

The leaders of free worlds, and I your President. We will pursue the 100% safety of all, not just our own or some. The sky is the limit, as the population grows, but the airways need to be safe & secure. With any Nation that can't respect our Privacy, who then will not respect us in any future, none alignments.

Don't feed the enemy. When you can just distract it, then obligate a tactic to all their surroundings, that let's them face their judgment day, from Terror Crimes Against Humanity.

As that, I urge us to Pray, Love & deliver Hope to one another. We make terrorists realize, their leaders are of wrong & destruction, as we are THE UNITED States of America to all the Republics, to which it stands. A New Golden Age.

God Bless to ALL & May our Father, Mother & Jesus Christ be with us."

The leaders who promote this thinking suppress those who want to do good so that the deceivers can stay in power because God didn't supply them with a position, or they "failed" to find it, strung up in wants instead of needs. Mike Johnson, our Speaker of the House, talks to God in a room of The People's Building. Should he? Should all Priests and all those who discuss testimonials of talking to Jesus and chatting about His presence? Should Lightdoers and Palm Readers across our country be considered unfit in society?

This is how YOU are mocked. You might say I am crazy, but are they all? Knowledge is power; the opposite of knowledge is arrogance.

That's why we separate Church from State: to ensure the government cannot exercise undue influence over Americans' spiritual and religious lives. Any current medical accusations that defy your well-being, light, or "assume" you have a purpose based on religion are unjust. They give no doctor or official the authority to extract you from public view. True light sees through illusions, corruption, and, yes, even "staged pandemics."

"Demon-crats of High Leaders, used Diversity, to set someone up that didn't know the job well, to not see past corruption of papers they signed or couldn't see, using Diversity, instead of Qualified people that are of diverse backgrounds, then attack the group exposing the lies."

- Lyle

False light creates illusions and upholds the current mainstream narratives. I can say that I am not false light.

"For we wrestle not against flesh and blood, but against principalities, against powers, against the rulers of the darkness of this world, against spiritual wickedness in high places."

- Ephesians 6:12

"And we know that for those who love God, all things work together for good, for those who are called according to His purpose."

- Romans 8:28

"Those who deny freedom to others deserve it not for themselves; and under a just God, one cannot long retain it."

- Abraham Lincoln.

We forget our own divine nature as gray skies form over our heads. We cry for help, hoping our hearts will soon be at rest. As we look up and see blue skies form, we see a light of warmth that shines to our core. Our roots strengthen with wisdom, faith, and hope. Our hearts open and expand like air flowing through troubled land. **Our hearts are the key that unlocks self-divine.**

Golden Rule –

"Do unto others as you would have them do unto you."

- Matthew 7:12

We shall feel no fear but strength. Those who teach, explore, and create a light of hope lead us to glory. To dig deep to find the core of a problem and fix it for one's value and self under God, Spirit, and Soul. We stand equally, not divided by one's success, but justified by one's beginnings for the light of opportunities given. A path we all shall seek.

"Truly I tell you, today you will be with me in paradise."

- Luke 23:43

God said, "These people claim to worship me, but their words are meaningless, and their hearts are somewhere else. Their religiosity is nothing but human rules and traditions they have simply memorized."

- Isaiah 29:13

"And I heard a voice from heaven telling me to write: 'Blessed are the dead who die in the Lord from henceforth. "Yes," says the Spirit, "they will rest from their labors, for their deeds will follow them.'"

- Revelation 14:13 (KJV)

Old ideas will not protect us anymore. We need new solutions to provide for us in a way that helps heal our species before it's too late…

Our hearts need love, which is the cure; those who show love shall be pure.

Note: This (*) means I am trying to comment and connect with you throughout the read. Example: *Could our Earth be Hell's realm? As we live here, then die to ascend to our pure self-destiny? *

Dear reader,

I am sorry if the way I interpret things does not agree with you. My main goal is to try to find a way for us all to become one again, as we used to be in the past. We need like-minded ideas, solutions, and people who have common sense. The one way for us to move on from bad-mouthing others about their skin color, gender, or love interests is to not talk about these situations or simply avoid conversations we don't wish to engage in. How simple...

Why am I? Perspective is not taught. I hope to change your light from dark to shine.

Do give us hope that someone can see. I am not chasing bad, nor am I chasing good. I am striving for all of us to love one another. I can only try in the way I know how. Please follow me on this horizon of open-mindedness. I am, however, taking what was deplorable on my path and making it prosper for those who are struggling. Turning the bad around for the better. We also need to learn that the Earth wasn't created for humanity to be a paradise but to work and serve each other, making a purpose.

I will explain my path, my mistakes, and others' mistakes and interpret my ideas, finding a way to merge them all with explanations from outside information as well. I will express my ways of writing, going back and forth. It is your job to listen to me and follow my lead as we break through the glass ceiling of our existence.

I cannot do this alone. If you judge me after this book, then...

Maybe I am not the issue. Judging me?

For trying to help us?

Who do you think you are to deny me?

To deny anyone trying to explain certain wrongs and provide a different outlook?

"If someone says something that is incorrect about a solution, it is the attempt to solve a problem, instead of relying on others who could not produce a solution or any answer to begin with."

- Lyle

Remember, it goes back and forth. This requires a quiet spot for your mind to grasp any concept. This is not a quick read during a break while at work, or a bathroom break. This requires all your attention. You need to relax, have a glass of wine (if old enough), or enjoy a lovely day in the hammock.

A lot has happened in my life. I just want to share the most prominent issues and learn some lessons as well! Note this: if you get what you want, that's God's direction; if you don't, that's God's protection.

YOU MAY READ.

"Write the vision & engrave it plainly. So the ones who read it, may run to it, as it may Tarry, it'll come at an appointed time." Habakkuk 2:2

Chapter 1: Part 1- Gathering Your Attention

"Remember readers of this book, as you can proclaim me as a Prophet, Philosopher or both. The quotes added in the book by me are signs that were given to me to speak."

- Lyle

If you are reading this after the intro, then I have captured your attentive attention. I hope to keep it and ask that you pass this on to a friend to read when you are finished. That is all I ask. I lost my old writings and am reconstructing them now that I am older. This story takes place in Upstate NY. I wish I remembered dates; I am sorry, I only recall some. It involves some travel, so please stay with me and find a connection somehow.

My story will not be like most. My explanations may feel like statements or confessions. I want to convey the idea of you trying to step into my shoes. We hear that expression a lot, but truly feeling this energy of light could be transformative! It could be true that certain names might be altered or omitted—this might be the first book without names, though a few might be listed. Mine is akin to a memoir. I refrain from naming most individuals because I don't want anyone to think it's about them. I simply want you to understand that I am not perfect, but there are many imperfections among others.

These events might be true, although they lack substantial factual support. I am doing this for myself and to help others. This will be a different read than any before. Who said a book had to be perfect? It can still be a learning experience. I want your attention to how I felt, not others'.

I am using "United Nations Equal Country" as a made-up land.

Words, actions, and character define your path. This is a book, and if you think it's about you, it is. Freedom of speech is a gift granted by our founding fathers in the Constitution, for which I am grateful. I may propose ideas on how to address current issues and support our veterans, though... who am I kidding? I am writing this for myself. Like anyone will listen. Everyone writes in a diary; I am documenting events that have affected and damaged me. I write as if I am sitting in a chair next to someone and talking to them. I express details that can be key to pointing you in a certain direction.

Many things have happened in my life. Some events are not meant for discussion, as those that do not matter do not deserve mention.

My first trauma, which I vaguely recall, involves my dad's brother—my uncle—who took me on his ATV to check traps on his trails. For some reason, I remember crying on the way home. Years later, around age 10, my dad and aunt recalled me saying that Uncle beat me, pinching my stomach uncomfortably and hitting me on the head. I didn't remember much until my aunt mentioned it before she passed away—a soul I dearly miss.

Special thanks to anyone in my life who made me feel like I belong. Most only put me down, assuming I would do something stupid to empower your unintelligent lifestyle. However, the joke was always on them, not me. Surround yourself with positive people for a more profound spiritual healing. If you cannot, fight until you can escape unexpected troubles.

Before I mention other things, I want to show something else that hurt me.

My second trauma incident occurred when I was around 11 years old. My grandpa and a family friend traveled down to North Carolina to visit relatives for what was supposed to be a two-week trip. We stayed another month because of the gambling stores, which I will talk more about later. My grandfather had won $5,000, which could only be withdrawn in amounts of $500 twice a week. On our way back home, we went through New York for a rest stop. My grandpa and his older friend smoked while I went into a restroom. An older man followed me in, claiming to be a friend of my grandpa's, who was also present. Despite others being around, he made me feel deeply uncomfortable and threatened to kill me if I said anything. I returned to the car, acting as if nothing had happened. I couldn't understand why it happened or why an older person would do such a thing. He tried to get close to me, but I dipped.

That happened when I was 11. Spiritually, I knew something was wrong. They say trauma opens realms for you to understand that something exists beyond.

"Heal the soul and open your mind to gather what we shall find." This was my motto from a young age, which I've carried with me throughout my life as a means to connect with my younger and adult self, finding insight from past and present experiences. Some lessons are good, some are bad. Healing your soul begins with addressing the troubles and suffering in your mind and gathering the necessary ingredients for understanding. I learned this at age 11, wiser beyond my years.

Chapter 1: Part 2- The Beginning

I remember standing on top of the stairs around 4-5 years old, and that is when I felt my first "jolting" experience—like almost gaining consciousness. It was a nice sunny day in the spring. The ground was wet, but days blur at that age. I definitely loved playing with my cousins that day despite that weird experience. We played games from Power Rangers to Hot Potato. We would fight and argue, but we were kids. As I got older, I didn't know why I wanted to hang out with just a few of my cousins. Yes, we might have started our own fire in the woods with sticks and dolls. Uncle caught us and had to pee on the twin flames, but back to my three cousins. They took the football and kept bashing my head in. They thought I told my sister about it when I went to grab a toy— I didn't want to burn anymore.

The headache was horrid. How I didn't black out is beyond me. I told my sister about it when I was crying, but she wouldn't do anything. She just said, "You're fine." Whatever, lol. Thanks for caring, I thought to myself.

One of my cousins who was involved, I ended up signing her name on our grandfather's garage. She got whipped for it. I did laugh... My grandparents lived next door to me; my grandmother passed away back in '07, so it's been 17 years. I wish she were still here. When she passed, I would always be outside, looking up. The word "Patience" came to mind as I would gaze upwards. Yeah, I would talk to myself, but we're all guilty of it.

My grandfather taught me one lesson; he used to do construction work and always helped with the lower ground stuff. His boss then asked if he would help with roofing. He took that step and realized he was good at roofing. Always take a step into something you didn't think you would do.

There is always a lesson… the result? You will either succeed or fail and then understand how to be successful when the life cycle turns around. Break it! Anywho ☺

I would always be looking up, sensing that something was there. One time, my dad got me a BB gun for my birthday. My older cousin wanted to shoot it, claiming he could kill a porcupine. I did shoot at him too, but I was around 10. When I saw him fall, I realized I didn't want to do that anymore. Though I didn't know God or His words well, I felt a sense that we should protect and have our Second Amendment. I don't agree with killing for sport. What gives anyone the right to decide what dies and just rots when it's trying to survive or enjoy life like we are? I agree with having it for protection and to get food, not for a killing spree. I noticed we humans know this but don't always follow it. We are civilized animals; some prefer to see happiness, while others want to kill animals because humans aren't on the list. We then go after intelligent animals in the kingdom provided by our higher power for food supply, not for sport. That was my idealistic thought at a young age.

I just wish we had more compassion, even at age 10. With that mentality…

I always knew I was different from others. I encouraged myself to find out the truth. When I looked up again to know what I needed to do or if I existed, I lost my grandma in the mix. It was the hardest thing I went through, as it was my first funeral, death, or even a sense of loss. That hits a child in an excessively big, unthinkable way. When I found out she had diverticulitis, the same as my father, sister, and now myself, the doctor cut her open when she was in pain on her right pelvic area. She died of sepsis. Malpractice is the one thing your biggest criminals are hiding in the medical field. Not all, but it seems like a perfect job for a serial killer, right? Do just enough to avoid suspicion!

Death is a part of our existence, but if longevity is brought up to our current technological times, I am sure it would result in cloning if you can clone an animal, which has been done by 13 cloning facilities—3 that I know of Takara Bio in Europe, Source Bioscience plc UK, and US Biological Inc.

"Cloning is suitable for replacing Donors for body parts, which may already be in stone."

- Lyle

I just wanted to ensure and give you insight that things are possible, because we should all keep our minds open to the "What ifs."

Remember your grandparents needing to take a lot of pills or just a few? I wish people would understand we have most cures. They take from your life savings just to afford medication that can easily be distributed at a much lower cost to keep you healthier. We all know this. After my grandmother's death, I came to realize we were legit just guinea pigs, waiting for the wheel to turn and whether we could keep riding. But once you fall off, that's it—that's Big Pharma for you.

Enough of that; I sometimes get heated and can ramble on, especially when I feel it very deep inside.

I just know memories are all I have of her. Her name was Helina. Trips to the beach, ice cream, cookouts, and gardening were her favorites. One time, a few more of my other cousins, sister, and I were with grams. She would watch us sing "Spice Girls" in the garage; I would also sing Backstreet Boys. We would dance and have fun. When it would be just grams and I going to the store, she would buy me a soda. I would have to guzzle it down before I went back. I was told not to tell my cousins. I did not.

There is a picture of me with my grandma, mom, and myself. She had these furry Disney dogs that were in it too. Sometimes, I wish we were young again. When you get older, you understand the "valued time."

I wanted to express these certain paths because I know we all have those little crazy moments as kids that we slowly remember as we carry out our lives, whether they are good or bad. What kids learn, see, or hear—they carry that like a chain reaction of what you put in the life bag for them to take knowledge from. We all go through a death in the family; if you haven't, just keep yourself busy and make memories with the ones you care about.

I want to gather a connection with you; I hope it is working. I want to expand your mind if you let me.

Throughout all this time, the school has been alright. There was this lunch lady that I would see randomly, and she would also look at me and smirk. I met this lady again when I got older. You will see that it also involves her kids. I had school friends, but I just did not really have friends to hang out with daily. I had a neighbor and whatnot, but I drifted apart. Really, I only hung out with family and cousins. I enjoyed singing and acting in school. Kindergarten through sixth grade was okay; I got held back in third but took summer school. I have vague good memories from third-grade field trips to Hartley Island and the Nature Center, as well as similar trips in fourth grade. In fifth grade, we went to Upper North Canada Village—crossing the Canada border was fun! A couple of kids took a pic of the agent, and he took their camera. That's a big no! I was also part of Hearts for Youth, an organization for kids to enact different ideas for fundraisers. We would work spaghetti dinners at a local church and volunteer to serve people. We also did the Iditarod because we read the book called "Winter Dance." It was great, especially being pulled by classmates pretending to be huskies while I was the leader!

In sixth grade, we went to Camp Wabasso, which was fun— simple team-building skills. In seventh grade, we went to another camp for more team-building exercises. In eighth grade, I think we went to Canada again and did rock climbing in an indoor facility. In ninth grade, I don't remember much, but in tenth grade, I ended up dropping out. It's whatever.

Why? Well, before I explain, let me get back to the story from when I was younger.

I always kept looking at the he or she on the TV screen, wondering if they would kiss a woman. It was something I thought

I would like when I got older, and later, it was confirmed that I did. Kids know when they are young how they feel or how to address themselves. I let others tally it up in their own heads. Others tally it up in their own head. Parents may think it's wrong, but it's not. Every parent has experienced something that went against "current protocols" or agendas at some point in their life. It's okay to love whoever makes you feel complete in your heart. We face judgments from every single person, yet we're told not to judge a book by its cover when we're young and to love others too. Was it okay for my cousins to hit me on the head with the football for no reason? So, do not judge me just yet.

The higher power (Jesus) wants us to leave judgments up to him, but we swallow our existence on apps, fighting and arguing with nonsense judgments about other people, knowing that we too will be judged. Every day, I still hope to hold onto the belief that something is there above us. Yes, there might be a lot of ignorance floating around, but I feel that connection of beliefs. We are doing an excellent job of separating ourselves with hate, when what one does in their household is not their neighbor's business. If you are affecting someone physically, then yes, you should help them. Once we separate ourselves from our differences and learn to compromise, the area gets better for all, not just for some.

We may be heading into a dark time where it's legal to marry who you want, but people will still be victimized. I support everyone, but as an openly gay man, I don't agree with pushing it in people's faces, being half-naked in Pride shows. When Dr. King fought for rights, they were dressed professionally, not as sexual figures. A person is defined by their character, not just their physical attributes. If you want to identify differently, take the steps to do so. Ensure you're not offending others; dress accordingly. A bearded guy in a pink twirl dress might get laughed at, not by me, but by someone who finds it funny. Be aware and careful. Our government could manipulate issues under our noses. I fight to prevent these tactics from harming humanity and those who deserve equality.

We are normalizing mental health issues. We are rationalizing them in an attempt to make all things seem normal. I firmly believe anyone who identifies as non-binary or uses they/them pronouns has a multiple personality disorder or is possessed. Period. If you are like that, you need to compromise with people around you so we don't judge each other. I never formally came out; people guessed. My parents never shared their coming out stories. Your sexual orientation and preferences don't need to be known unless you're comfortable sharing with someone who wants to discuss it.

I once worked at a job where this person was a girl, but changed her name to a guy three months into the job. I got yelled at because his first name was a girl's name that stuck in my head, the legal name. He changed it. What you need to do is, before you go work any place, establish your identity. Do not talk about it and go about your day. When I see people transition, they always go way beyond a chill demeanor and make it well known. In other words, exaggerate yourself to the point people question you.

All parties can set aside the correct laws needed. Just do not be over the top, too sexual and you will be simply fine! These are small steps to ensure us all of Equality. Heterosexuals have the same laws sexually. No public nudity, males could not use the bathrooms with females' vice versa, but again, most pride parades, not all, are half naked, and this is something that does not need to be. We should all walk together, Equality of all colors. Orientation?

There are only two. You are either gay or straight. Let me explain ☺ There is a reason I am saying this. There are only 2 genders. It is not the rest of the world's job to acknowledge what one does to your body. Why let your community be your business? As some would bring forth laws banning certain ideals. Then you underestimate someone who does not agree with you. Do not set yourself up for failure. If you do not like what someone is doing, you are judging them. Do not allow yourself to be judged. Again, I did not ever come out. It is no one's business about your sexual life. Our pelvis decides the sex. When someone dies, with a skeleton, how do you think the investigation figures out the bones to be male or female! This is where you do the fact searching about our body's, before making another gender. When someone dies, they are going to not have any evidence that you transitioned yourself. DUE TO PELVIC DIFFERATIONS. PERIOD. DON'T argue. Because it hurts. I know. We are all hurting, do not forget.

For the ones who feel unwanted, this is for you!

Romans 12:16 states, "Live in harmony with one another. Do not be proud, but be willing to associate with people of low position. Do not be conceited."

First Amendment: Congress shall make no law respecting an establishment of religion or prohibiting the free exercise thereof, or abridging the freedom of speech, or of the press; or the right of the people peaceably to assemble, and to petition the Government for a redress of grievances.

Marriage Act: Due to the Bible, it is falsehood and not against the law. If or so what a religion says. This act is now unjustified as I am a "We the People" taxpayer Ordained individual who knows. They make laws, thinking people will not challenge them, so let us make unconstitutional laws to make people "think" they are laws. That is why we now have the right to get married in all 50 states. Half the reason I became Ordained! Thanks to our Congress. The Marriage Act was unconstitutional due to them making a religious-based law.

I had a dream where I was floating around town with a plastic waterbed. It showed the town to be underwater, due to suffering. Everyone in the town is hurting. This results in an overflow of emotions in our societies.

THIS IS HOW WE FIX THE DIVISION. The LGBTQ should keep the abbreviations, but I understand putting terms on a name to understand what it is. Oh, a label. Why spend your life labeling yourself?

"Be who you want to be, not push to be."

- Lyle

"Demon-crats of High Leaders, used Diversity, to set someone up that didn't know the job well, to not see past corruption of papers they signed or couldn't see, using Diversity, instead of Qualified people that are of diverse backgrounds, then attack the group exposing the lies."

- Lyle

Please understand that I am not trying to divide anyone. I am of this nature. I tried to dabble with my crazy crying friend once, it was not my thing. Throughout life, I have felt bad, due to others still saying God hates us. But why doesn't our constitution allow all of us to be killed then? When it says they cannot make laws based on their beliefs. It must be a whole cooperation of all RIGHTS. If it does not reflect harm on another.

Homosexuals: Sexually attracted and/or romantically driven to the same sex.

Lesbian- A woman who likes another woman & a butch who is considered dominant.

Gay- A man who likes a man

Bisexuality – A person that likes both sex

Transsexuals – I talked to several on an anonymous level. No proof, whether they believe it or do not. I do not care.

Often, a person still likes the same sex, or a straight guy will dress up as one and use the gay agenda to arouse himself in public, making the gay community look bad. Not all who are gay do this. Some enjoy wearing lingerie. Some cross-dress but prefer the same sex over the other.

Some want surgery, some do not. Some dress up but still have intercourse with both women and men. So, what does it matter? It only matters to you because that is what you presume within your heart. Do not impose your views on others who do not agree. Those who do not agree should also refrain from giving opinions that are against others' way of life. Two wrongs do not make a right. Compromise needs to be reached now before it gets out of control.

You are all labeling yourselves! One term describes it all: homosexuality. I am not being invasive about this. It is about understanding how we are dividing ourselves based on labels. It's like calling yourself a label for a shelf. If you still don't grasp the concept, then you will face judgments from uninformed people in society who lack the brainpower to accept differences but still nag others for presenting their sexuality at home. No one should care; it involves two consenting adults. Period.

I left out "Q" because, again, it aligns with the same meaning. The real meaning? Odd or unusual, but as a collective group. You are doing it to yourselves. Also, why are we discussing bathrooms when we should be focused on doing our business and moving on? Public bathrooms are not your home closet to express opinions; they are for releasing bodily fluids. Period. We can simply use designated areas and avoid conflicts. It's really THAT simple. Yet, some insist on making their preferences known. Use and leave!

For some reason, both sides of the aisle prefer conflicts with no consideration, only what fits their AGENDA. Haven't we seen this? Most agendas sway back and forth to suit political parties. I urge us all to stop this. There are other societal issues that require greater attention, which I will address eventually. The time is now to align with our own resolutions. For those who cannot understand, I hope you will someday. We are all being manipulated for political purposes. The weak-minded are exploited and expected to depend on the system. Why do you think it's difficult to save money on income-based housing? It's because the government keeps people dependent to secure federal income. We are too focused on others' perceptions of us and not on finding our purpose or the right job that would make us and others happier. We are not born to be lazy or to let others dictate what they should think of us. But go ahead, continue to do it to yourselves. At the very least, I warned you about the political schemes. I would appreciate it if you understood why I said all this. Keep your sexual intentions to yourself unless both parties consent. If you're having a comfortable conversation with someone, then so be it. Take a break, cool down. Chapter 2 is next.

"Taking action, showing a lot of work or little, can still gain you the communications to process your next upgrade of paths unexpected decisions to align with your experiences & to what you still need to learn as you grow. Instead of being indolent, expecting things to come unnaturally."

- Lyle

Here's a quote from a Golden Girl, "I don't know how people can get so anti-something. Mind your own business, take care of your affairs, and don't worry about other people so much."

- Betty White

And I say, be who you want to be, but be mindful of others as the world navigates these changes. Not everyone will agree with you, just as not everyone agrees with me. As I said before, do not judge others for their differing opinions; it doesn't make you any different. Let it be.

PLEASE DON'T GO.

"No President, Justice Judge, Federal Judge nor Lawmaker from any State, can't change the marriage act that allows ALL equal, to marry. No matter the orientation. Those that try to abolish it, will loose, and those actions shall be deemed your resignation of hidden bureaucrat agenda that won't work, as it's not for the peoples interest, but stir the pot." - Lyle Light

Chapter 2: Drop Out Adventures

Prior to earlier discussions, I dropped out because, in 10th grade, my mother was diagnosed with stage 3 cervical cancer. They didn't know if it would go away because the stage almost progressed to the 4th.

I thought my world was collapsing because she told me this the summer before school started. I wasn't always good at attending school and missed more days than the average person. Around this time, I was involved in a few select choir musicals: "Annie," "West Side Story," and "Jesus Christ Superstar," which was my last.

I went to my guidance counselor and the principal when I was upset. Four "friends" made a fake Facebook page about me, degrading me and my family. They told me who they were, but I could have gotten them in big trouble. My counselor knew, but I let it go. I wish I hadn't.

Every day, it affects me. When I think about the past, I try not to. The very friends I thought I had turned out to be fake. The funny part? When I was 14, I took a hit once off a bowl with my cousin and her friends. It was one time, no effect, just to take the pain away.

The fake friends who did that to me? They ended up at one of the girls' older sister's apartment complexes, and I was invited too. She would buy us underage kids beer or vodka a few times. They would smoke weed, but I never touched it, nor cigarettes! I had this tendency—I liked the way my mouth felt fresh. Who wants to kiss someone with smoker's breath? I've tried, I gagged. (LOL)

As you see, when I describe something negative, I try to toss a little positive in there. They would smoke cigarettes, and I thought it was gross. I don't know why I came, oh yes, I was invited to a party and felt noticed. I can't tell if they spiked me. I fell down the stairs, so they say, and I was lying by the apartment door, getting hit in the head when someone walked in. They would go to the other sister's apartment nearby to find food and come back. They waited until I woke up to help me. In my head, I was like, "You were invited. Maybe it could have been my fault?" Even though I was only 14.

I would like to highlight another factor that affected me during the challenging times with my mother and "friends." While I was in Select Choir, a situation arose with my music teacher. Once, when I was supposed to go on a choir trip, she mentioned that the guys didn't want to room with me. She also couldn't place me with the female students because I'm male. Firstly, as a teacher, I believe such matters should be handled by the superintendent, not directly by a student. When I confronted some of the guys she mentioned, they denied saying anything of the sort. This incident was the final straw for me.

Academically, I struggled with math and found science and Social Studies okay, but I loved gym and music classes. After confronting them, I didn't show up the next day. I spent two weeks straight in my room, only getting up to eat and drink before returning to bed, battling depression.

Before leaving school, I had already been working two jobs to support myself. After dropping out, I took on a third job. That summer, I decided to ignore judgments from others who may not understand the challenges I was facing. People often dismiss our traumas or exaggerate our responses, but I strive to highlight the difficulties people face in sharing their truths.

I'll also touch on another friend I encountered crying in the school hallway. Looking back, I realize I should have left her alone. It's a lesson to remember: if someone is upset about another person and you don't know the full story, it's best not to judge. Walk away if it doesn't concern you—Not my monkey, not my circus! I'll share more about her later; she was there for me when my mother battled cervical cancer for the second time. I'll expand on that later, turning a negative experience into a positive narrative.

Back in high school, I had two teachers from sixth grade walk me home once because one of my cousin's friend's older brothers wanted to beat me up. I ended up punching him in the nuts once because he thought he could push me aside. Calling the teachers was his first strike. The second time was on a trampoline at my cousin's house. He tried again, but I managed to kick him down once more. I went back into my cousin's house, and he was furious. The asthmatic, unintelligent bully seemed to hate me simply for being myself. I've noticed that guys who are deeply averse to someone who is unafraid to be themselves often avoid covetousness due to envy or jealousy. Aside from him and those incidents, that covers most of the bullying I faced in high school.

After school, as I mentioned, I juggled almost three jobs: retail, restaurant, and as a personal assistant. I'll elaborate on the personal assistant job later, likely in Chapter 10. I want to maintain your interest in my storytelling, avoiding any pitfalls I might encounter.

I'd like to add something for employers. If you're a retail business owner, consider letting your employees pick a favorite item to promote. Track how many customers buy their chosen product and incentivize them accordingly. This approach can help employees develop communication skills, sales tactics, and customer relations. They'll sell something they genuinely like and understand—a strategy that encourages product knowledge. After all, if you like something, wouldn't you want to learn more about it? #TeamBuilding... This concept can be applied in all retail settings.

The primary job that gave me the most hours was at the Kilp-Inn, where I started helping my mom, who was the housekeeping manager. My dad would pitch in when needed, though I never paid much attention to his exact role. I suppose you could call him the maintenance person. They both worked there since I was eight years old, until I was about seventeen or eighteen.

My mom had a heart attack once at the Kilp, and after her first bout with cervical cancer, she faced it again, needing surgery.

Despite this, I continued working. I started by washing dishes at the Kilp while still assisting my mom. Occasionally, I helped with food preparation and the cold line (salads and desserts). My boss often came over right as I finished portioning salads and desserts, nodding in approval. It was a satisfying feeling seeing the boss appreciate the work of his employees, including mine and everyone else's.

However, when it came to working with my sister, she brought all her emotions into the workplace. Note to self: working with family can be challenging unless you fully understand how they behave or treat others under pressure—a valuable lesson learned along the way. One day, I met a girl interning to become a chef, a year older than me. We became close work friends, and I'll touch on her briefly in future pages.

I made a mistake during my time there. When I was 15, I took $100 that was left out on the counter, thinking someone had forgotten it, but it was actually meant for change. Can I note? I was cleaning at the time, and the old saying "finders keepers" came to mind. I'll delve more into this later. Before that, I felt guilty about it when the bartender manager asked me, and I lied. I was young and didn't handle it well. Remember when I mentioned "Jesus Christ Superstar," the musical we did in school? Well, while helping my mother in one of the rooms, I found a Bible and read the part of King Herod, the role I played. He mistreated Jesus because he believed he was lying when, in reality, he was jealous. That's what I took away from it.

During that time, I wanted to explore other career avenues beyond restaurants, so I attempted to obtain my GED. Unfortunately, the night class was canceled due to insufficient enrollment. Consequently, I secured a position at the Waive-Edge Hotel, overlooking the Thousand Islands—a charming and enlightening experience. My role primarily involved front desk duties, with occasional bellman responsibilities if needed. I genuinely enjoyed my time there.

As the summer drew to a close, I encountered a memorable incident: a naked bride was discovered outside her room. My manager humorously noted that this had been a recurring event for over seven years—an amusing glimpse into hotel life. However, since it was a seasonal job, I was eventually let go and moved on to the Stones Anchor Hotel, a new establishment in the area.

At Stones Anchor Hotel, I kept a low profile, listened attentively, and absorbed as much as I could. What excited me was that they used the same IQ Ware system as my previous hotel. I performed well and even unofficially trained a few colleagues due to the assistant's negligence in her duties. Ah, the joys of minimum wage jobs, where those in higher positions often take advantage of incentives while pushing their workload onto others—users everywhere!

Around eight months into the job, the true colors of my coworkers began to show. One memorable incident occurred when alarms went off, leaving two new hires at a loss for what to do. Guests started calling down, unsure if it was an accident or an emergency. Frustrated by the lack of direction from the manager on duty in the kitchen, I took charge. I instructed one new desk agent to gather guests in the lobby while I teamed up with a new hire to investigate the issue—one that involved a pressure release on the third floor affecting the pool area. I swiftly relocated guests while firefighters addressed the situation.

The next day, my hiring manager questioned why I hadn't provided cot beds or accommodated guests in larger rooms despite my efforts to upgrade rooms for families. It was disheartening to prioritize guest comfort over protocol, yet I remained silent as I aspired for a promotion to Front Desk Supervisor. Despite my dedication, the General Manager cited my lack of experience as a setback, especially during the slow period following a room flood in March 2015 when I was just 18. It seemed an ideal time for training and gaining experience in the hotel industry, but opportunities were missed.

I tossed my uniforms and gave my two weeks' notice. Within that time, I stumbled upon some information: the Front Desk Assistant left her email open with my name typed in, complaining to our boss that I was annoying her despite her giving me orders to follow. It was unbelievable—getting criticized for the extra work she pawned off onto me. Wild. To top it off, my sister's girlfriend went to school with her! Small world, indeed. I later found out she was a snob in high school. I'm glad I got out of there.

During this period, my mom underwent chemo and radiation treatments. I couldn't handle everything that was happening. Treating me like that while my mom was going through such a tough time? It was also my parents' anniversary that same month. My sister and I split the cost of a room for them with a Jacuzzi, around $100, with my discount. I used another worker's ID number to refund the amount back to my card—a big middle finger!

After the first scare, and then this time? I thought I was going to lose a parent, you know? When she went for surgery and made it out safely. The doctor gave her a 25% chance to live! My friend, who was crying in the hallway at school, was around when my mom returned. She stayed with us, and I stayed with her at her grandmother's, though she didn't know. I couldn't stand being home with my father, so I hung out with my friend instead. Until I caught her talking badly about me on her phone—she would turn off her data when staying with me because her grandparents were bigots. I thought we could just crash in my room, sharing a bed, but then I saw the text where she admitted to using me until she found something better.

The same day, she brought her stuff back to get washed, and I drove her to work because she had her bag packed to refresh. Guess what? I didn't pick her up after work like I was supposed to—I left her there. I was the only one who never judged my friends. What did I do to deserve such mistreatment for no reason? She even called me fat to her friend despite being bigger than me. Okay. This girl even purposely gave me an ex-lax bar, pretending it was a candy bar... As we went to a beach one time with an ex of hers, his brother, and her other friend. We went to a store beforehand, and she secretly bought it to "joke" when that is considerably dangerous and could be labeled as assault if I had any colon issues, but hmm.... Diverticulitis results in over constipation if too much ex-lax consumption. How long was she doing that, with me not knowing? Need I say more? I knew she and her friend were trouble because the day before I left her, we were at her cousin's place, and her friend tried to get me to take money from her purse he'd seen. He blamed me after he took it. That's when I knew these were not the best people to be around.

So, I said screw it. I went to Florida for a guy, which lasted for two weeks. I thought I might stay, find a job, and have someone like me for me. Turns out, it was a quick trip! He turned out to be faker than those dating ads you see for ChristianMingles.com. You'd think chatting with someone for a month would lead to something, but there was no relationship there at all. Not my fault—he started acting weird once I got there.

When it was time for me to come home at the airport, my 5th-grade teacher was unexpectedly there! She offered me a ride back home once we landed at Syracuse Airport. There was an older lady with her two grandchildren who overheard me talking to my parents about contacting them upon arrival. She heard me mention the town name and said, "I'm going that way. May I speak to your mother?" I agreed, and she said I sounded like a "good boy." She would have given me a ride if I hadn't already met my teacher. They owned a farm; the older lady was sweet, and her grandchildren were well-mannered. I enjoyed the window seat on my flight back very much!

My teacher gave me a ride after we disembarked. They dropped me off, and that was that! I truly believe everything happens for a reason—especially my mom's treatment timing and running into these helpful people at the airport. It felt like a blessing. Once back, I worked in retail and another hospitality job, holding down two jobs to save money until I could afford my own car!

I financed a car through a bank since I had no credit history— I was considered a ghost in the system. It was cool because I got a low APR, around 8%. The car payment was $240, and insurance was $100—not bad for a Toyota, and it was company-owned too! One of the jobs was at a dollar store, which was alright, though they could improve their inventory system to avoid overflow. I liked my Hispanic boss; her accent was great, and she always tried to make us laugh.

I remember a funny incident when a customer said there was a "contrite spirit" way in the back, and my boss ran out fast, leaving my manager shocked with a "What the Heck" expression. The next day, an older gentleman was found behind the aisle where the laundry detergent was, stripping! I'm glad I wasn't there to see that—I only heard about it.

I had considered transferring jobs down to North Carolina near my aunt's place, but when I visited, the store was so disgusting that I decided against it. They were always backed up on trucks, and the aisles were a mess. The floors looked like they hadn't been mopped in ages—it wasn't worth the hassle. When a company has money but can't invest in their business, it shows greed with a lack of motivation to maintain standards.

That was my first and then my second job, as I was working two at the time, as I said. At the Candle Flame Hotel, the hiring manager liked my resume and started me that same day. I liked that but understood at some point; true colors are shown! He would use incognito on the company computer using Craigslist Chronicles. Imagine... When I left there because of the hostile work environment, the GM took the housekeepers' tips and used them for pizza, etc. That is wrong! I heard one of the sales ladies even cussed her out! While the inspection was coming, she was taking down all the stuff the owner asked her not to do. Who would want to work in that behavior? Of stupidity. Abusing power because that is what makes little managerial peasants feel better about themselves. Legit! I am sure you have been in that type of scenario. (I quit the dollar store because the GM said I was acting too tired and gave me a choice: "This job or that job." So, I resigned from the store.)

I did enjoy some of the guests; some were genuinely nice. Some were staying a while. One paid me to walk her dog and take care of it while she was gone. I do not think the GM liked me being that nice. She would give dirty looks, though she would say she was not! When I confronted her about it, one day, one of the workers would show up smelling like pot. I ratted on him because it was that bad. Then, one of the manager housekeepers lied and said I gave a guest inaccurate information so she could write me up. I guess because I mentioned she violated the others' rights by taking their tips. Then, a guest called, saying I called myself the manager, which I never did. One day, I was heading to work. I had this weird feeling to write my two weeks' notice. I didn't have enough time, so I went out and got .25 cents.

My manager and the GM wanted me in the office to fire me for those reasons. I ended up giving her that quarter and expressed the line from Uncle Buck: "Take this quarter, go downtown, and have a rat gnaw that thing off your face." The mole on her face could legit make a mole egg. Yeah, I judged her. I did apologize a few years later when I was out grocery shopping and ran into her. She said, "No one has ever done that, apologized for anything to me." Hmm, I wonder why? Taking attitude out on employees is not ever a good thing. I hope she turns her character around; deep down, there is an etiquette person. Making your team feel unworthy to make your business any money should not be what your team feels. There was this one older lady they used for the night audit. This was one of the reasons why they were letting me go; I will share it. I was trying to hold back not to, but if I am writing this, I better explain it all.

I fell asleep behind the desk off to the right. No camera was able to face in that back spot. The night auditor came in to replace me. That's why I lost the dollar store job. The GM held onto that and used it to her advantage so she could get her family member behind the desk. Why? To deceive you? Plus, do you see how the GM got me to quit my other job to control the situation? Then, she fired me when she knew she could better hire a family member whose last name was different from her married name. That's why she hired her.

After that, a friend of mine offered me to do a singing contest. It was like "The Voice" but with a more local setup, without the buttons and spinning chairs. I said to myself, after dealing with all that extra nonsense, I wanted to focus on myself. I sang a short 30 seconds of "One Step Closer" and got through the auditions. We had a country night, and I sang "Johnny's Daddy." The week after, I did Uncle Cracker's "Follow Me," and then I sang "Lean on Me." A week after that, my elimination round was when a guy sang the same song first—"All of Me" by John Legend—and messed up. So did I. He caused it by messing it up first, I think. My slight idea of bad juju for that song. Lol, then I was eliminated.

I was 7th out of 33 that started! I was excited about that.

As I mentioned, I enjoy singing. It makes me feel whole, you know? I also create art or crafts occasionally when I'm in the mood. It helps keep the mind flowing, especially when you drop out of high school. I then tried to get my GED a second time at Water City High School. I was there for a month, but then the board said I wasn't in the district, so I couldn't take it. My cousin, who was a teacher there, tried to help me get in. It sucks, but at least I can say I tried again. I was staying with my sister at the time.

While I was there, I started having weird dreams, like something strange was going on. I remember when we were younger, my sister had a cellphone and said she had a weird experience, like floating above her bed. My dad blamed it on the frequency. It seemed like an out-of-body experience because that's what I felt. The area was grey and black, with something in the corner of the room. My body couldn't move; I heard a high-pitched sound, and it felt like I was entering inside the wall. I was getting lifted above the bed and struggled hard to free myself. I fell onto my bed and woke up feeling like I had just fallen!

One job I had, I remember putting dishes away at the Kilp, and I heard a voice say my name. I asked the servers if they had said my name, but they said no. I heard the same voice during my experience—OBE, out-of-body experience. When I tried to lie down again, it wouldn't happen. It only occurred around the same time of year, at the end of summer, twice. The second time was quick, floating around and then back down.

I shared this with my cousin when she came to visit, and she said she had experienced something similar. Her, my sister, and then me—weird.

I've learned a lot from working through the jobs I've had since my first one at the Kilp Inn. I say that because one time, my aunt visited from North Carolina for vacation and suggested I should come down there if I ever wanted to. I had some money saved for my car payments, insurance, and phone bill. I explained to my ex-boss from the Kilp that I wanted to borrow a little gas money to broaden my horizons by going down there. I was just working part-time at a kids' store, nothing major, but my last paycheck wasn't enough because Aero was closing. My car tire popped, so I had to use some of my funds to fix it. That's why I decided to ask him—it's okay to ask; you never know the answer as long as you pay it back.

My sister and I once took a three-day weekend trip to visit family in NC. It was fun until we got lost in this small town with road signs that had horror movie names like Jason St., Horror St., Myers St., and I think another was Chucky St. It was freaky! The point of this is she had a lanyard hanging with her picture from the mirror. It was her work card. I felt weird like I would see myself wearing something similar. Anyway, I gathered my belongings and decided to venture out of my comfort zone to see what would happen. Venturing out of your comfort zone tends to give you a better sense of life.

So, I packed up and decided to see what moving had to offer. I was driving to get gas before heading home to say goodbye. I really just wanted to up and move. First, I had to get a new tire for the right front because I hit a curb, and it went "POW" so loud that

I thought my whole car had broken. I had to drive slowly for about 10 minutes, feeling like my car was wobbling because the tire was close to coming off the rim, but thankfully, the rim wasn't damaged. If that's happened to you, I'm so sorry, that's not fun! One of the guys from the store came out and took my car in. This was around Christmas time, so I hoped they would give me a deal. They cut me about $20 off. I only had $100 from what my old boss gave me. I left his house and headed to the gas station for all that to happen! Ugh. It's okay; I stayed positive. (FYI) I had $150 to go on. I didn't mention my wallet had a secret compartment with $50. It was a Christmas present from my parents. You'd think I wouldn't forget that! But it was a sigh of relief! I ended up with a full tank and still had $130 to spare. My car at that moment only took $20 to fill! She was a beast, being a Toyota. I was able to see the scenery of Pennsylvania, riding into Virginia—a nice cloudy sky with sunshine warming inside, not needing any heat. The valley of the hills on the 81 looked like a Bob Ross painting, with the green leaves and some scattered in assorted colors, like autumn was around Christmas time. I enjoyed every minute of it.

Knowing I dropped out and went through all I went through—emotional, depressed, and not trying to be obscure about others' intentions—I felt a sense of release as I was able to feel free. We are somewhat free by nature due to laws and free will from God. I think the Goddess is nature, and we are here to figure out how to survive and keep the earth pure. I took this trip to allow whatever higher power existed—whether you say God or Jesus—to guide me. Both are separate, but I always hear people talking about them like they are one. Technically, I would say we are all Demigods. Earth is the Goddess, and God is energy. The two sons became our guides through the Yin & Yang process of evolutions within DNA and historical preclusions.

This is my thought process as I travel further down to North Carolina, but I must stop and do a couple of things. I'll be right back.

PLEASE DON'T GO.

Chapter 3: New Ideas & New Scenery

I was driving through the end of Virginia into Durham, North Carolina. The warmth was kicking in, reminding me of my trip to Florida to see that one guy. I had to take my jacket off because it was getting warm, but it was nice out. I forgot to mention that the guy who sat next to me on the flight was a bigger guy, but I didn't see it that way. I felt safe, even though I was a little young, 17. Sitting next to him, I felt like he might be a U.S. Marshal. I wonder if there's a policy that allows young flyers to sit in the back on United Airlines or other flights. I don't recommend United Airlines; they use an exceedingly small plane.

Anyway, back to the drive. I saw a few people with signs asking for food or money, which struck me as odd. I thought about how we could help world hunger, yet we have a system that is more concerned with what it can get in return. When veterans are on the street, some of these people are vets. I do understand how some take advantage and find a hat or gear to deceive you, but this was someone older who looked like a vet. Why have our military and government failed the elders who battled? The higher-ups sit in their offices with no battle scars, just more policy laws, paper bills, and PR stunt smiles. Imagine that.

Seeing the hills, trees, and beautiful scenery, I felt bad. I get it; some people end up homeless due to their own actions, but we can prevent homelessness and protect our vets. I figured out a solution!

1 Peter 2:20 makes this promise: "God will bless you if you have to suffer for doing something good."

Veterans, this is for you and the homeless!

Find land, get it bought by donations, or get a grant by supplying the land with produce and solar lights that will provide free electricity. This will save money and give you investment returns! We have so many elites and top figures. Put the money where your mouth is. Failed leadership has let this happen.

Take the grants and investment returns from the solar company and/or agricultural (USDA). We can have local contact companies come in to volunteer with tax relief to provide good humanity to the community. We can create small homes or a big facility. It takes a village to get something started. Afterwards...

People who apply and already have funds can contribute a small percentage towards the place. Those needing an old folks' home, with family consent, can also participate. If they have life insurance with no families, they can put their income into a vet/homeless fund to keep recurrences going. This fund can access needs, such as those contracted by a bank, and you can charge a rental fee for a vet member bank and civilian bank all in one, so elders do not need to go far, and the area is still making money.

You can set up a non-profit organization or enlist volunteers who know the business to find the benefits these people can receive. If we have shelters for animals, why not humans? Are we that disgusted in our hearts? By doing this, people in the healthcare industry who were fired for not taking any vaccines can apply. Set the homeless and vets up in a big building, like a gym, to hold them until it is processed what they deserve.

Once the homes or buildings are done, offer an online site and gift shop. People can come in, see vets, and hear stories with fees to visit when there are events. Offer internships to show others how to be human with morals. You can have land making money from produce, with the residents and some of their families earning incentives by participating in family planting events. Use the VFW for those who want to sign up for membership. Offer a reasonable 6-month or yearly payment to become a member, which grants you access to the VFW bars. Civilians wanting to help can get free produce up to certain limits- three times a month.

Additionally, the military could use unused buildings on their bases. If they house homeless vets and others, they have the supplies to help until the buildings or homes are built. Other current members could also donate. While they stay there, their benefits could be helped. To save money, military members, who are paid on the clock 24/7, could be used for these types of services, using resources wisely.

Other incentives for civilian memberships could include discounts on ticket events, gift shop items, a free tablet from the government, and other benefits we can set up, like sleepovers with the elders for an admission cost, etc.

Then, local poverty-stricken areas can benefit! Those who can supply small donations can come twice a month to grab fruits and vegetables at no cost, just whatever they can give. This will help distribute food to hungry homes. Bigger companies toss out fresh food daily, wasting billions of dollars. The only time I see communities coming together is if someone with a well-known last name gets hurt or passes away. The rest of us get shunned to the boonies. Do not tell me I am wrong; some will agree with that statement.

This is just a small start to fixing the problems we face. You are making money while supplying fairness with food. God gave us land with food. Did the dinosaurs pay for food? I am not saying all food should be free; it should be just enough to help those who need to eat to survive, even if it is just an apple, orange, or banana. You might be that person's only way to get food for the day. Why starve them? God put fruits and vegetables on our land for us to eat, yet millions die from hunger.

"Demon-crats of High Leaders, used Diversity, to set someone up that didn't know the job well, to not see past corruption of papers they signed or couldn't see, using Diversity, instead of

Qualified people that are of diverse backgrounds, then attack the group exposing the lies."

- Lyle

"If there's stories of dinos with Tribes, should be a sign that we've been told something else."

- Lyle

People who get ticketed for feeding the homeless today? Guess what? We can start investments in stock with the right broker and keep feeding the homeless while making money to beat the system with tickets. Most police are tax collectors anyway.

Some do not even realize they are prisoners of their own jobs. Acts of good to humanity get trampled on by unintelligent minds all over our current system. They could walk by and not do anything. They do it for empowerment but "blame" the law. While they are walking around seeing who is getting fed, they could stop a theft, carjacking, or someone driving while on their phone, passing pedestrians, pedestrians using hidden parking lot areas for car sex, drug deals, etc. Instead of turning into the park, they watch someone feeding someone and turn away; instead of going into the park, where a person could be there to cause harm, using the black night as a place to hide their car and bags after a murder.

The AAP (Academy of Pediatrics) Is financed by drug companies, and so are medical schools. Vaccines are doubled in the US prior to 30 other countries in the Western world around 1990. As Vaccines are the largest division of the Pharmaceutical industry. What I'm asking – Similar to Jim Carey & Melissa Mccarthy's note, no kid was dying before 1989 of drastic diseases when 26+ vaccines came out. Greed. Greed. Greed. So we ask not to look at newborns for money but to take a loss for the good of Gods children.

We need health officials who don't look at us as a hamster wheel of guinea pigs. Other pharmaceutical workers and doctors are slowly coming out. As the people that run drug companies get money through grants, shareholders, etc. So, who has to pay them back? The sick who come down with diseases given. Why so many chemicals in our food? To then create and find medicine to relieve it, when you come down with something that triggers the cancer cell we all have in our body.

Your body has the greatest Immune system, but when unknown vaccines are being shot in a baby without a parents knowledge of all the ingredients, it is bad parenting. Trusting a science that owes money back to shareholders. It's just another food for thought. This is just the tip of the onion layer of hidden greed. Instead of focusing on medicine that works with natural born diseases. Not man made. Like Corona (covid), the bad Chinese lab. That made good Chinese people look bad. To find out who's for money, not people? Those of leaders who take out shareholding of a company that they complain about that makes a cause? Because it would be conflicts of interest but lie to our face. Once they run for an elected position. Those who are trying to fix it? Will get blamed. As they aren't a part of the stock/shareholder. Most of the medicine is also made overseas from China & India. You get sick through bad chemicals in food, then take medicine. Imagine that.

-Author

But they make sure to fine people with silly tickets because they do not want to die of starvation, being homeless, or a vet who fought for YOUR rights. This is the repayment they get. I mention solar lights. They are going to be essential in a blackout caused by sun flares that will interrupt current radio and cellular networks. The power connection to the grid gets cut off! All homes are dark. We can survive off solar panels when this happens. Some do not even realize that. Why not try to prepare for an outcome, even if you think it is silly? If we have solar, we can cut off gas stoves to

53

free electricity. That is the number one way to cut emissions! Then?

The government can help homes save more money installing solar grids. They can pay half of what they pay now every month or pay it on a yearly basis so that homes can save more money! Farmers use this to help with the cost of taxes, wages, and insurance.

Solar panels need photonic crystals, diamonds, and spruce pine quartz to help cool them down, as the electricity grid is good till we can figure out how to make solar panels 100% effective without a blown panel when it goes. As we need more spruce pine quartz the finest quartz to date.

It is not about asking for "free" things. It is about understanding that if we have resources so easily given to us, why is it bad to ask to help poor families save? Without thinking about your people like a pyramid scheme of suppression and control against the fundamentals of being human.

Remember: Oil cools our earth, and so does gas. Fundamentally, we will always have water. It replenishes itself like oil. Yes, some areas can dry up, but we have enough water to sustain for years. Water and oil replenish themselves through tons of secret reservoirs within the earth's layers. Could we run out of oil and gas? If so, this results in Antarctica fully melting, and sea levels would rise 200 feet, if not more. So, if we want another pole shift, that will occur if we do not act now.

Also, cellphone network towers are an energy form that sustains RF energy. It affects our bodies and can cause health risks. Look it up. When you raise the RF or data to G or faster services, it holds on to radiation, like your phone or microwave. This affects our population's health and lifespan, increasing genetic damage and cancer. I stay off my phone as much as possible. It is like we are test subjects. Phones keep us distracted from becoming something good ourselves. I am doing this instead of liking a silly video or a picture of someone you will never meet. Have you gotten the concept yet?

We can get the best scientists and builders to figure out the right dynamics. If we use all the gas and oil in our Earth, it will become a moon. That's why I am mentioning solar panels. It isn't too late to fix this. We still have time to reverse it within the next 70-100 years. Why not fix the issues now to protect the future? Or just wait until the last minute? This isn't me giving false representations. These are real possible outcomes!

"Harvesting Oil or Gas from our Earth is the analogy of the Alien Mothership taking Energy from the Earth. The real aliens are humans profiting from and running oil companies cracking our earth, Thinking we won't run out of resources. Look around..."

- Lyle

The top of a car's hood, front to back, supplied with solar panels, is enough to power a car for a long time. We do not have this. We have plug-ins. Doing that, plus only using gas when the battery is not working, is fine. I guarantee that all the world's wealth can be carried out. In this case, you would be going to gas stations less and saving more money. Why do you think they are covering more of the sky with fake cloud chemtrails? So, it is hard to produce energy from locals now that many are getting solar panels. At least, that is the way I see it. No one will buy enough gas to supply the gas business fund. Why would our government take away the most substantial financial substance of their income besides taxes?

The average person will say that is not possible, or the car guy at the dealership will say it, too. Us humans, all we want is to have more and more, followed by a variety of things, instead of what is needed. Most of the time, we drive to get away, enjoy adventures, or go to work. We also just eat to put something in our stomach so we do not starve.

55

I find it funny when people go out to luxury dinners, spending $100s to $1,000 when they are not saving money. They are spending poorly, again, just to fill a belly. While someone out there just wants a sandwich or a salad, they are riding the solar bus that is getting free energy. But that person starving cannot receive any energy. See the wrong yet? We help technology companies but neglect our own people.

A homeowner of 30 years would end up paying around $25,000 or more for electricity. As a solar panel costs that much. If given a solar panel, switching from grid to solar. Homes would have electricity in not just blackouts, but stormas and hardships if you couldn't pay, oh right, couldn't pay. So they can't just shut you off like they do now.

Hebrews 13:16 says, "Don't forget to do good and to share what you have because God is pleased with these kinds of sacrifices."

A lot of political figures who say they preach forget about what they preach, making laws that require them not to do so. The 11th Circuit Court of Appeals officially ruled that feeding the homeless is a protected right in Alabama, Florida, and Georgia. So, those getting currently fined should keep them and write to the court, then send them back! All states are violating this if so, as it is protected by the 1st Amendment. Other states could adopt this issue or any issue that reflects better judgments on all humanity.

If anyone has an issue with what I said, then you are the reason this world is greedy. Period. It can be done in the right spectrums of deliverance. This is all I thought of at that moment, seeing that from VA to NC as I was rolling into my aunt's driveway. With a low tank, I said, "Screw it," and went to the gas station down the road. I figured I would refill again so I wouldn't have to worry about it later. My grandfather once told me to always make sure you keep your car filled at a half tank. Pretend the half tank is empty. It works if you have the cash for that all the time, but I was down to $110. Cheap gas in NC. It was like $3.05-

$3.10 in NY but $2.69 in NC per gallon. I got a Hershey bar when I was done pumping, which is my favorite, by the way.

This was a 13-hour drive! What made me stay awake? A Monster, coffee, and two 5-hour energy drinks. Wow, I would not recommend doing that! When I finally got to my aunt's, she had gone with my uncle. They went on vacation to the Butterfly Mountains. My grandfather and their family friend who was staying with them were there too. My grandfather lives near my parents in NY. After my grandmother died, the one I miss deeply, he sold the house and moved to the hill next door. He goes to NC for a vacation to get away from the cold. Boy, he is a smoker nerd. One after another! My golly! Yet the doctor says he is healthy.

As I got in, I said hello, hugged him, and said hi to the family friend. I had to go lay down and sleep. My face was vibrating; my body was jolting, but not in a spiritual way. It was almost like an energy drink attack. I slept like a baby! I felt refreshed when I got up. I ended up making dinner for us. Grandpa took out a hamburger, and I made some delicious patties. I used garlic, a little salt, pepper, smoked paprika, chopped dill pickles, Worcestershire sauce, and onions. Exceptionally good! After dinner, we cleaned up, and I went back to bed.

The next day, my aunt and uncle were back home. She is married to a Mexican, and he works in masonry. He is particularly good at it, too! Honestly, one of the best. My aunt works in the kitchen of one of the colleges, serving the students. I figured I had to find a job, so I decided to look. I found a cellphone store that paid biweekly. I said, "Screw it, I will try it." I put in an application, and he hired me the same day. I then took home a paper describing the difference between CDMA and GSM, which stands for Code Division Multiple Access and Global System for Mobiles. It is a two-network radio wave system used by wireless carriers. Certain phones through CDMA can only go through Verizon or T-Mobile, while Sprint and AT&T use GSM. Knowing the difference is important because, on the computer, you have to put in which one. If you put the wrong one in, activating someone's phone would mess it up. After I learned, the owner gave a test to make sure you were following and knew what to do.

I also had to make ads through Craigslist. He was strict about how we supplied that. It had to be written a certain way, and certain things had to be listed. This made sense, as we were trying to market the store. Mind you, this was a small phone business. I would drive back from Hillsborough to Raleigh. Once I was there for a month, he gave me a key to open or close. I thought that was cool. He had one employee who would come in late and just slug around like a sloth. I don't think he took his job seriously. Then, he said the owner still owed him paychecks. I guess he would take money out of his checks because "he felt the need to," based on how the employee was working. Not my monkey. The owner ended up firing him after hearing our conversations through the camera. As I didn't care to know, he was just telling me about it.

I guess the owner was going under. He had multiple speeding tickets and got his teeth fixed with white porcelain teeth; he would always brag about having them. A lady came in, complaining about her service. It was not our fault she kept her data off and didn't realize why she couldn't get service. He would say, "You keep eating that stove of food. My teeth are white. You look dirty. Get out of my store." I sat there thinking, yes, she deserved it. After a while, he used his teeth to disown someone. He looked like Humpty Dumpty without the king's doings.

If someone has to use their own features to be crude to someone, then that shows where their insecurities lie. The point of being crude is not allowing others to see your insecurities; that gives someone knowledge of what to use. Period.

After that day, the boss was vastly different. He acted like I could take charge if I learned more, but he would still be upset with customers and rude to them. I decided to hand in my two weeks' notice. He had us sign a contract in the beginning. Afterward, he said that in the contract, we signed a two-week notice policy. If we did not inform the boss in enough time for him to hire a replacement, it would result in the suspension of our last payment of work. He legit just stole my money, adding in an extra clause that was not there before so he could keep his money and not pay the employee. ME.

I said to myself, I guess it does not matter where you go. People who open a business think their ego allows them to treat others the way they do not want to be treated. Why? Why must people be this ignorant?

I do not talk to one of my aunts and uncles back home because they opened a produce farm. I would put flowers on my grandmother's grave, and now they have a store. They ripped my flowers up to put theirs there. Then, they bragged on the internet that they do this every year just to boost their ego through their business. See why I do not talk to them? It's the same arrogance as the porcelain teeth mobile store owner.

After a while, I was able to save enough money to pay my aunt and uncle for whatever they needed. They charged me $200 a month for staying there, which I thought was a good deal. I had to search for a new job, but since I was home, I cooked, cleaned the house, and made sure my chores were done. For fun, we would ride up to the plaza and stop at one of those gambling game rooms in a storefront location that I mentioned before. You would think they would be illegal! Nope! They are fun, though; you must be 18 years or older to play. My favorite one was a Native American slot with wolves on them. I did not win much, but I liked the game. The flutes and raindrops they used in the music felt near my soul.

While looking through Craigslist for jobs, I found this marketing company that dealt with a telephone service, AD&D Subcontracting Company – Third party, as a solutions provider. I thought it was a paid weekly or biweekly type of job. Nope! It was straight commission. Legit. I figured this was not for me. For some reason, out of 20 people, 7 of us got picked. I was one of them. After I applied and had my interview, I was picked, which I found exciting. My gut did not like the commission part, but my spirit said stay, so I went back for the orientation about the product to learn it.

AD&D was putting fiber optics in the ground to supply faster internet service. Technically, it was clear quartz crystal used inside, a layer inside the cable that transmitted faster communication. Most phones have it and a small percentage of gold. Clear quartz is used as a frequency-controlled product and uses a high vibration frequency. Imagine that! They use it in watches, remotes, radios, and most technology. Some say that's what the pyramids had on top of them. We shall never find that out, but till then, the company had you defame Clock Warner Cable & Network. They were using copper lines, which are used for short distances. That's why most people experience an outage or interruptions of service. It was also a shared network system; at least, that's what they were telling us. They used that as a marketing tool to show that your privacy was not secure and that a virus could get passed down to each circuit line. Look up more into crystals. I use them in meditation! You would be surprised!

"Kids under the none working legal age, should not have a phone, due to data leaks and other entities guilt tripping your kid. SO unless companies create a kid safe only phone, with a law in stone to protect Gods innocent kids."

- Lyle

Anyway, fiber optic lines are good for long distances. The company also bought a TV provider, Jerec TV, that used satellite. They told us they spent money on the receiver that connects to the space satellites. Clouds still got in the way, but we had to sell them on the fiber optics. They offered decent prices. You get certain commissions with certain packages. If you sold just the internet, it was $50, the same with the phone. TV and Internet got you $100. With TV, Phone, and Internet, you would get $300. I thought it was crazy. Could this be? As he was explaining this, my mind went into ponder mode. This is what Big Pharma does: it uses people to sell pills legally and gather a big income because doctors use us to buy the medications at a regular pace of consumption. If I found a legal pill gig, I would take my selling skills there.

I thought of that because cable and the internet are addictive. If you do not have service, you ask the next guy, "What's your Wi-Fi password?" If someone does not have their pill, being an old person, they would go ask the neighbor, who they know is 70, and just go for a refill. At least the cable is on to watch Jeopardy. See my point? Everything is controlled by money. Doctors do not make the pills. If they did, they would be cheaper. Let that sink in. (Remember this when I mention a hotel in future pages.)

What does that do for TV providers? They charge random fees on the bill or raise your bill after a year when they already make millions every day or month. Keeping everyone at a minimum low is reasonable. Nope. Greed makes them want more. Ugh. Because we had to have a retention number, the customer could call at the end of the year and complain to get better service. I met this guy who was ex-army and worked in my hometown on the telephone poles. Small world! He showed me the ropes. I figured, from the stuff I thought about vets, the man upstairs put me with this guy. Though I did not ever share my thoughts, I had this weird notion that if our government knew about the small information I believed to be true, they would most likely get rid of me instead of doing what is good for humanity. I am sure we have a lot of bogus positions that could be weeded out, like I said. Save us more tax money!

Anyway, the guy training me gave me the intro after my boss gave us directions. I had to do my first knock.

"Hi, my name is _____; I am here with AD&D to explain why we are digging up near the end of the driveways. If it has not been seen yet, we also want to explain once you see them digging. We are here because we have found a faster way for you to experience your household needs. I can tell you are spending $200+ on services. With us, we can cut that by $80 for a while. No contract." (Then find something to relate to once you acknowledge why you are there.) I then said, "Is that a Syracuse blanket? I am from Water City!" He said, "Yep! My family lives that way." Boom, I got the sale. It did not happen like that all the time. Some were mean.

But what have I learned in life? Anything you sign with a date and your name is a contract. Paperwork for your taxes, doctors, therapist, receipt, etc. is a contract! Most do not get that.

I had one issue with a customer because he was closer to the transformer box that held the entire service. He tried showing me his meter level for download and upload speed. His son was there, and he was drinking. I could tell he was getting belligerent, thinking I was lying, or was it our company? I tried to leave his house, but he ended up attacking me. My hand got stabbed with the pen I was using; it broke, and I was bleeding. My hand was just covered in blood. I should have tried to put him in the ICU, but I did not believe in violence. I called my boss, and he told me to come in or report it. He suggested walking it off. Technically, I could have sued him and made him pay. He was drunk. Alcohol affects people's minds and may imbalance their attitudes. I did not judge him for that. If he was sober, I am sure he would have been different. I walked it off and did not say anything to anybody besides my boss.

As time went by, I came across this college professor who taught English Literature. He allowed me into his house to explain services; he bought but then canceled. I think of him occasionally because he is the reason I wanted to author this book. I had tried to draft a book, I told him, but I did not finish it. I lost my writing when I was younger. (Our family cat tore it up.) So now, I rewrite my inner traumas and forward emotions here, as you just read some of them. I had to go through more in my journey. I was not mad he canceled. OK, I was a little. I thought about it more, but in the professor's house, he put a pad in my hand with a pen and said, "Start writing."

He said, "There is no wrong way or right way to set up a story. If you have a meaning of substance, purpose, and a greater outlook for one to perceive in one's path that allows them to carry something you can talent yourself to offer for another to succeed, you do not get anywhere with just yourself. Temples were not built by one person."

I started writing at his kitchen table while his wife asked if I wanted leftovers. I said, "Sure." I began writing about how this all began. Years later, I still think of him. What did I learn from this? No matter who you meet, be kind. They might teach you something about yourself you didn't know you could do. Some are here to help us rather than mislead us with incorrect information. Thank you, sir. I forgot your name, but I did not know what you taught.

They fed me, which was cool. Another couple, a bit older than my grandparents, were also customers. After I provided them with service, they asked if I wanted to join them for dinner. We went to a buffet, and they paid for me too! You meet good people if you are caring. One more customer who made me feel whole was an older lady from whom I got another sale. She had a picture that resembled my uncle, who passed away when I was little, and she looked like Helina, my grandma. Her kitchen had tiles behind her stove similar to my Grammy's. It made me feel at home, protected, or like I was on the right path. She was sweet and nice. After the sale, as I walked out and looked up, I saw a cross in the clouds.

After all that, I was the 4th top employee out of 7 other locations, which was surprisingly good. I had a couple of bad weeks because some people didn't want to switch, or I couldn't make any sales. I tried everything, so I went back to Craigslist to find a second job. This company wanted someone to do personal errand work. The conversation was strictly via email. I gave them all my information, and they sent me a check. They wanted me to cash it and buy toys for church... Okay, I thought. Then, they asked me to cash the check at a well-known bank. I deposited a $2,000 check. It turned out to be a scam. I kept all the information on them in case anything caught up with me later. Ugh. A guy came by my aunt's place saying he was looking to repossess my car. I packed my stuff, didn't tell my boss at the marketing company, and left for NY.

I will cherish what he taught me about seizing opportunities and gaining experiences. He bought "The Outliers" for the top 4 of us who were left out of those who couldn't earn commissions—a book about those who are different in the world, figuring out how to apply deep understanding of something so fragile: us. The scientific term for an outlier? A phenomenon outside normal experiences. It's an informative book that I would recommend reading.

I couldn't bear the thought of anything bad happening, so I went to three different police stations and called 911. They took my information but didn't take any action, even though I explained that I had unknowingly deposited a fraudulent check. The officers said they had received similar complaints from others. I went home feeling frustrated and unsure of what to do next.

It's unfortunate how companies and individuals deceive others just to elevate themselves. Some seem to get away with it for a long time, especially if the right people aren't investigating. These experiences reminded me of several scriptures:

- Galatians 6:7 – "Do not be deceived, God is not mocked; for whatever a man sows, this he will also reap."

- Proverbs 16:13 – "Righteous lips are the delight of a king, and he loves him who speaks what is right."

- 2 Corinthians 8:21 – "For we aim at what is honorable not only in the Lord's sight but also in the sight of man."

- Jeremiah 9:5 - "Everyone deceives his neighbor and does not speak the truth; they have taught their tongue to speak lies; They weary themselves committing iniquity."

- Proverbs 11:18 – "The wicked earns deceptive wages, but he who sows righteousness gets a true reward."

- 1 Corinthians 15:33 – "Do not be deceived: 'Bad company corrupts good morals.'"

I learned a lot during my time there. I used to sing in the car on my way back to NY to energize myself. When I returned, my mom was happy I was back safely and that she's now cancer-free after surgery. I found a job through someone she knew on Facebook, working at a gas station called Gas Trac. I thought, why not? Although I'll miss the Southern weather, I enjoyed my trip back through NY, stopping to see the White House—a historic building that stands as a testament to our nation's history and the presidents who've shaped it, even as temporary occupants.

On my way out, I drove under a long, dark highway underpass that felt unnerving and claustrophobic. The narrow highway made me acutely aware that one wrong move could disable my vehicle. It reminded me of the importance of safe driving habits and being vigilant of others on the road to prevent accidents whenever possible.

We can take a break now. First, I need to figure out how to approach the next steps. This is where I start to see some revelations. Oh, remember when I mentioned my sister and her work card on a lanyard? Well, guess what? I ended up having the same thing—my picture on a lanyard. Could that have been a premonition? Nah, I prefer to think I'm just crazy enough to understand my path!

One more thing before we move on: do you remember my cousin who accidentally hit me in the head with a football when I was 18? On his 21st birthday in 2015, he started serving in the Army. But way before that, when he was about 19, and I was 16, his mom went to a local fair where she met a Palm Reader. The Palm Reader gave her address and phone number to his mom (I wasn't with them at the fair). They told me about it later because I was in the car with them when his mom visited the Palm Reader a week after meeting her at the fair. When we arrived, my cousin and I stayed in the car. His mom went in, and without seeing us, the woman knew there were two people in the car. She told my cousin to come in and asked me to stay in the car. Over the next two years, my cousin struggled with what the Palm Reader had told him (that he should join the military within a certain timeframe). The reader also predicted his mom's future success, saying she would "fly high" after earning her GED.

It's important to be cautious about what information you trust. As God says, "Trust in me, and you have the power to navigate through troubled lands." With a good team and calling on his army of light workers, we can uncover deceitful practices that serve dark purposes. The power of the people manifests in many ways. Let's help each other—that's all I advocate for.

"White lightdoers with good charm, may you be free from harm. For good you must do; united we stand. Take darkness back to its devilish land. May goodness prevail forevermore, banning darkness and standing tall with our Lord," said Spirit.

May God protect our troops in all branches of government, both from foreign and domestic threats!

PLEASE DON'T GO.

Chapter 4: New Start, New Sight

So, you remember that friend of mine that I left at the store for talking crap about me? Well, as I am getting started at another new job, she makes another appearance. Golly, just great...

At the start of the new job, they had me go to the corporate office's main location for orientation. I went, and it was fun. They start you as an assistant manager – just a sheep, nothing more. Not even a free meal! I didn't even get lunch. They make you sign a contract, giving up your right to challenge them on labor rights and violations. We need a policy that makes it criminal for companies to make contracts that try to override the State Labor Authority.

You'd think they would do something about that kind of stuff. Again, with the deceiving! But that's just me, I guess. Anyway, I was thankful I got the job, but I didn't take many breaks, as they had us working 40-50 hours and sometimes almost 60! The boss would give you a weird look if you asked for a break.

The girl my mom knew from working there was all right and cool. However, she came off as condescending and thought I was, too, as she was the Assistant Store Manager. So, we had a heart-to-heart to get along. Loved it. We laughed and even tried CBD oil one time. We tried to get each other mad or say things we normally wouldn't to see how we would react. I wish I had some of that! It was great. Made us focused and energetic! The cool thing about working there was that I was able to learn a bit about how they operated. When you have a membership card, and it doesn't work, it is not their fault. It is the main location having issues with the servers. One time, a guy came in and called me a "faggot." I told him he was a *phat* piece of crap and that he was banned. He did not come back again! Lol. Do not be rude just because an inconvenient situation got you upset. That's just ridiculous! Because it did not work for him to receive a discount on gas. So, Yin Yang, my friend!

While I was improving myself, I got offered the position of night shift manager, and that went well. I was always getting my tasks done – cleaning, restocking, and helping customers. One night, I had to take out the garbage during the winter. The last bin was further out towards the road, and next door was a salvation store for clothes. In the snowbank, I found some Canadian money! I took it to the bank, and $125 was like $90-something in converted currency.

I thought it was cool. Finders- keepers, but this time it was legit. No one came back to claim it. I held onto it for a week. Then, after I came home from the bank, I found out my mom was talking to my old friend - the girl I found crying in the hallway, whose grandparents are bigots. Well, she wanted to apologize and be friends again. So, tax time came, and we spent time together. She had just broken up with her ex, and for some reason, I cared, so I offered my support. We went out to dinner. My treat. The next day, we found a place in River Town, and then we called it an income-based place. I said, "Screw it, let's do it!" It was $600 a month for two bedrooms! Who knew? Looked nice, too. The first year was good, but during our first week there, and the first two weeks and forever after, she brought pot into the apartment.

I didn't want to smoke, but she insisted, saying things like "I'm tired of smoking by myself" or "Don't be a baby." So, I did it. Then, I turned into a pothead. I was still working at the gas station, and the local police and state officers would come in for coffee refills and stand there, taking a break. A bunch would show up for coffee and snacks at the start of their shift. One sheriff, whose name was "Officer Frotteurs" – *need I say more?* – would always say I was a good person, randomly at times, as he walked out the door. Lol!

During my time at the apartment and the job, my boss bumped me up to the kitchen manager. This was around springtime. One job, two years, and promoted twice! I had been there for six months before my friend and I cleared our dues and moved in together. This is the second year. Not much happened in the first year besides turning 21 and having my first bar drink. It was a bloody dragon – pink, green, and delicious! I can't remember what it is made of.

We would play pool and occasionally go over with the parents to my sisters' and girlfriend's place, which was just two minutes from the bar. There, we would again play more pool, darts, and smoke in the back. Just having fun!

I ended up getting a beagle dog as well! She was my world, still is, and always will be! She was shy, and my coworker's daughter, who works at a vet, was sent to the area where she was left in a garage due to a military family leaving, according to the report. They left her there. I don't know if anything happened to them about it. She fears thunderstorms. It's so hard to break her of that. Puppy pads do work, FYI. Best $200 I have ever spent! Her name was Bella.

Things were looking up; I had a cookout at my parent's place. One night, my dad was drunk. He said, "I could do better for myself." As if having a car, job, and apartment weren't good enough. He was jealous. They could never afford a car for themselves.

They worked at the Kilp Inn. As I mentioned, it was their last season there. He always suspected my mom of cheating on him. They would drink every other night, blaring music, which often led me to miss school. I admire my sister for being strong enough to deal with it all. They never saved money, yet somehow, I managed to save up for my car. I always had to take them to places. I remember when I was young, I asked for a $300 portable game player and cried and cried until my mom spent the money. As I grew older, I realized we could have used it for better things. My dad would insist he provided me with a roof over my head and demanded money for it. He called me ungrateful, but I was only 8 at that time. I never felt cool until I got the Gameboy, and suddenly, other kids wanted to see me play. Lol! However, that didn't give him the right to demand things from me years later, especially since they always asked me to buy them cigarettes and beer. No wonder I don't want to be near them!

I left to go back home with my roommate. We then saw our neighbor outside crying. I thought, "Please don't let this be another moment like my current friend from the school hallway." I will just tell you now – yes, it was.

Our landlord asked us, when we moved in, to let her know if we saw anything. We let her in and smoked together. We walked into her apartment, and it looked like a garbage dump. Her kids were playing on the floor. One was eating a donut that looked like it had been sitting there for a while. She had two kids: a 4-year-old and a 1-year-old. Her 4-year-old daughter wasn't dressed appropriately either! The father was in another state. I can't remember which one she said because they had broken up.

While we were inside her apartment, she wanted to smoke in front of her kids. "No, you redheaded dummy! They shouldn't see that." I wish I could have said that, though. But I didn't. Instead, I let the landlord know the next day. We had to pay off our rent. I taped it to a red balloon and put it in the hole of the door. It was April 1st, and the landlord got a kick out of it! I would try to spook her randomly at times.

Our landlord was funny and shared her first smoking experience with us when I told her about the neighbor smoking in front of her kids. She said she thought she was dying the first time she smoked, and when she went to see the Doctor, they told her she had smoked too much but assured her she would be fine! Lol. She was too stoned. She said she didn't smoke after that. Hmm, sure. Lol.

She then proceeded to inform us that she was leaving us when we handed in our rent. She had to move to another building because someone got fired. She knew the tenants there better.

The neighbor and my roommate's nasty friend got along so well that she was now babysitting her kids. She's using our Wi-Fi, too, by the way, without my consent, even though it's in my name. When we first moved in, she knocked on our door – forgot to mention that earlier – and asked for our password in exchange for $15 a month. She paid for a whole year upfront, which was cool.

The new landlord came in, and she was cool, too. As long as we followed the policies, she was all right. She had to manage two places. As I was getting ready for work, I let my dog out. Something told me to look up, so I did. I saw a cloud shaped like a dog bone, and next to it, a dog-shaped cloud. Just as I tried to take a picture, they vanished. I took it as a sign. She likes playing and loves her treats. I put her inside and handed in our rent again as a month went by. I got in the car. The landlord told me to give my boss papers to sign for my hourly wages for recertification. She didn't ask for paystubs, just written proof, which was cool since I didn't know any place to print off paystubs. I just didn't want to do that work. I heard sirens go off, and someone got into a car accident by hitting the light. If she wouldn't have interrupted me, I might have been in a head-on collision. Timing is everything, folks! As I left, she randomly said, "You're a good person."

As I worked my shift, time flew by. I was standing up at the register when a guy getting gas came in and said, "Did you see that guy?" There was this PC camera next to us with a screen, so I went to watch the surveillance footage. It showed a naked man running! My coworker and I thought he might have been caught cheating with someone's wife, as there was an apartment nearby.

After my shift, I walked around the apartments and noticed a van parked sideways. How did anyone else not catch it? I do not know! The back door of the van was open, and inside was a girl who claimed she had been kidnapped. She looked drugged, and I saw a needle on the ground. I called my coworker, who dialed 911 for me while I kept watch, pacing in circles to ensure the guy didn't return.

The police officer arrived, and I told him I wasn't going anywhere. He began questioning the girl. The guy had fled through the back woods, wrecking the front end of the van, as to what we could see from the damage. She told the police officer that he dragged her from her apartment into the van. Today, she's now sober and doing well, and they caught the guy that night at a diner; he turned out to be an illegal citizen. Knowing I helped save her that night made me feel good. The police officer gave me his number and offered to install a touchscreen radio in my car. He knew it would fit since his old personal car was the same as mine. The next day, I was working the day shift, and he came in and installed it while I worked. He was a good soul!

I think I can help our Police Departments with an insignificant change that could lead to a big, good outcome.

We have too many people dying of drug overdoses.

Police Department, this is for you! But I am writing this for myself, in my diary, as you will not listen to me if I come to you directly. Because I was the one who anonymously delivered those seven paper grocery bags with eggs, bread, soups, and water for seven families, along with a Gift Card of $5 each. It feels good to have done that.

There is nothing that says it is against the law to make a policy that gives individuals from the community free tablets, gift cards, etc., for reporting illegal activities or crimes. Choose compassion over obedience in certain situations where you see facts support that choice. To take out the drugs?

A policy should be set in place where all those individuals convicted of drug charges are automatically placed on a watch list. They cannot set up any cell phone or communication device through the intelligence agency. They must stay at an address with random probation checks for one year. If they owe someone money or if someone owes them, they will find a way to message them. All serial drug addicts also receive a tag for monitoring their whereabouts, like illegal immigrants. If we have free government phones, why not offer them to the immigrants when they are passed over illegally, as well as to those waiting for asylum or already granted asylum?

Each device can be tracked. They think ditching their IDs would help, but they will not know the fundamentals of how we use our technology when they see a free tablet, etc. I don't agree with handing them anything. Like I said, that is a way to use resources to keep track. Our constitution does not say that drugs cannot be policed more strongly.

"If our United Equal Country wants to combat drug crime, is to
follow the path, & submit a weep through the roots of the
system, as the Constitution doesn't protect Drug Violence nor
Drug offenses that kill others & by all means strips you from
Free Will & Privacy, until the drugs killing people faces a end &
those who Speak Truth shall face small consequences to those
actions, as Jesus died for ALL sins, but did not for drug crimes
against humanity, thy too, shall & will weep in purgatory."

- Lyle

Our judges? Last line of Humanity's Defense. Everyone, including our political figures, can come together. I am sure investigations are underway involving many people. But if a policy is being constructed for or against human rights, it is the small steps that lead us to the destruction of the destructor.

It is our duty, the people, to enforce the law against unethical leaders. As taxpayers, we command those in authority to act justly. Petition and undermine your corrupt predecessors. Restore rule and order in our communities. As the state says, we will get more money from tickets if the person repeats his crimes instead of keeping us safe.

Wouldn't that mean the current bail reform is now considered unconstitutional? They have repeatedly violated due process through the law. Therefore, the old bail reform should be reinstated or amended to fit and serve the rights of protection in communities. Those who are not in favor should be removed for allowing crimes against humanity. Period!

We can fix these issues. It just takes a minor change to deliver. Our current intelligence could be named the Federal Constitutional Bureau. Lower certain positions in this facility that focus on policing all those who uphold the law of our constitution. That way, crimes against humanity and other drugs or human trafficking are caught. I'm sure we have resources for this. At least, I hope so. I'm just trying to figure out why you are allowing all this chaos yet acting like heroes when you have the right to protect!

2-3 judges from every state and 2-3 police departments in every county/state have enough power to make changes to our fundamental lives for the better. Other agencies can follow behind them. It's about who will uphold their duties to protect from foreign and domestic threats. This includes elites, politicians, celebrities, all branches, etc. No one is above the law.

I mean, if we lived in a free country, wouldn't all laws be the same in all states? I really hope you think hard about that. I'm not trying to act smart; I'm just offering ways to fix issues beyond the talking points we see in politics. They use these issues to keep pushing agendas every election, making you think certain issues are arising. Because the animals running our stages are afraid of peace, every state should have equal rights across the board. Period. That will fix a lot of issues. Adopting the same laws within all states would ensure correct law & order. Back then, our Kings and Queens ravished death by cages and prisoners. Think hard about that, too. They still do today, but it's all secret societies. Yet they say I am nuts! Now, I want to add a couple of quotes I like.

Proverbs 13:20: "Walk with the wise and become wise, for a companion of fools suffers harm."

2 Corinthians 13:11: "Finally, brothers & sisters, rejoice! Strive for full restoration, encourage one another, be of one mind, and live in peace. And the God of love and Peace will be with you."

1 Timothy 6:9: "Those who want to get rich fall into temptation & trap & into many foolish & harmful desires that plunge people into ruin and destruction."

If they address conflicts within communities by seeking a flow of natural procedures where officers promote fairness, accountability, and equality of treatment, along with inspections and audits, these steps will help us all.

Again, we need like-mindedness, fair competition, and comprehensive trust and values for our nation.

If that upsets you, then the law should rebuke harmful individuals because the constitution is supposed to protect us from danger. I do not know all, but you must weed out from the bottom up, not top to bottom. Otherwise, you will be creating a missed entity that would recreate the same belligerence as before.

I am just trying to help.

Period.

The sheriff was done installing the radio in my car. I gave him the money he asked for, and he allowed me to split the payment in two. It was only $100, and he installed it for free. It makes you wonder, did he spy on me? We shall see in the future. Nothing has happened yet! Lol.

After work, I came home, around mid-April. The roommate was supposed to be babysitting the neighbor's kids, but when I arrived, she was sleeping while the kids were up. I ended up playing with them because the babysitter was asleep. "Wow," I thought. What a horrible thing to do. These are kids and you need to show them respect and attention! I woke her up, saying, "Wake up, dummy."

I started playing with them, and they were playing with my dog too. We started running around this playpen since the apartment had two openings on the side, you can run around from each room. I hit the darn toy bin with the side of my foot and ended up having to go to the ER room. I broke my foot. Yep! Sure did!

The ER doctor set me up with a month of therapy for my foot. It involved stay-at-home exercises with this long green stretchy thing you used to stretch with. I took it home, and then I shared with the neighbor what I had seen coming in. I don't care who you are; if you are not doing something right, I will make it known!

She got upset with me and said, "Why didn't you tell her before?" Hmm... I don't know, I was in the ER. The first week went by, and it wasn't on my mind. I guess that's why she was upset. I explained to her that her kids were okay because I took care of them. So, she was upset with both of us. Despite that, I still feel like I did the right thing by ensuring they were happy and well cared for.

I was out of work for a month, did not have PTO, so I went to the Department of Social Services, and they offered to help me pay rent. FYI, it was around $800. I still haven't paid them back. Oops! Someday, I will, when I have more funds to just give away like that. One day while sitting at home, I decided to go to the store to get some snacks. My roommate also had a job. She was working at the same dollar store where I used to work in the past. The manager recognized me from my time there. Occasionally, my roommate would use my car to get to work, often when I was asleep. Without asking! One time, in a rush to get to the store so she could make it to work on time, I bent down in an aisle and felt a sharp pain in my back – BOOM. My back cracked and I fell to the floor. No one was around to help. My back was so sore that I was crying. I held it in, went up to the register. "Are you okay, sir?" The worker asked. I replied, "Yes." She kept giving me that look, "Yeah right." I legit made it back to the apartment, but it wasn't easy.

My roommate/friend left me hurting. I was lying on the floor the entire time. She came home after work. We ended up going to the ER, well two of them. The first doctor thought I was faking and didn't perform any tests. I got a second opinion, and the doctor confirmed I had strained my muscles. Yet the first one thought I was faking!

I wish we could weed out unethical doctors by nurses speaking up, saying, "Certain doctors aren't following protocol. You are now released from duty." Simple! But instead, we will allow them to do as they please, at least some of them, not all. Anyway...

As the days passed, a month went by, including birthday. We didn't do much for my birthday as I turned 23. I didn't do much for my friend's birthday either. All I made for her was a booby cake, and we smoked and had some of her friends over. I didn't know them, except for what she'd mentioned and seeing them around school. That's it.

She baked me a pecker cake! Lol, but that was about it. I didn't have many friends who would come over to have fun. It was mostly her friends who came over. I talked to people, but there was this chick I met at the Kilp Inn that I was thinking of inviting. My roommate said, "I don't like her," and called her fat, even though my roommate wasn't any skinnier herself. Lol. So, some of the friends I did have were hers. She prioritized her wants over mine. Sound familiar to any of your friends?

So, I spent time with her friends rather than mine. I ended up giving her friend's brother a buzz cut on my birthday. He was one of the three kids of the lunch lady. There were 3 of them. One girl brought her boyfriend too, who was a well-known drug dealer, as they described. They would pack the bong and I saw white residue in it. After taking hints and seeing that, I said I was tired and wanted to lie down. As this was getting around 9 pm. They teased me, saying I was being a baby. So, I smoked it and felt very stoned. As they were smoking dabs as well. I continued to stay up.

I could have sent a message to the police officer who gave me his number. I did ask him the day he was installing the radio, if I could get my current friend in trouble by bringing drugs into my apartment. He said I could but I never did it, as I did not know the outcome of their behavior. My "friends" would want my roommate to take them places with my car, making me an accessory. Great. Nothing has come up in my path yet. One of the brothers of the friends mentioned that having a police officer put a radio in your car means you are being investigated. They picked up weed from a guy with my car and said that in front of him to scare him.

Anyway, after my birthday had passed, I was getting ready to go back to work. My job wanted to fire me because I was hurt. I saw it in an email my boss forgot to delete. Like the hotel situation, I gave my two weeks' notice, but the regional manager wanted to just fire me instead of accepting my two weeks. They tried to use minor issues against me, like not changing gloves, not throwing away outdated food from the hot box in time, and mixing the coffee creamers. Little crap to fire me, because they thought I was a liability due to my foot and back injuries. I shouldn't have told my boss about my back when he asked if I was doing all right. Why ask me that if you're being two-faced? Oh, just to get rid of me.

So, on my last day, the regional manager let me finish my two weeks because I mentioned that our contract allowed it. After I left, I made them $20 short by giving myself free gas! When I asked to see video proof of these accusations, there was none!

Companies that treat you like a carpet full of stepped-on minions deserve every missed dollar that gets abused out of their financials. If that upsets you, I do not care. I felt the same way working at the Stones Anchors Hotel. Wouldn't you?

So, now that I'm done with that place, I'm jobless. However, I did request my 401k, which had only $800 in it. One day, I asked my roommate to deliver the paperwork to the post office because I needed to get it processed. Guess what? They never received it. So now, my car is set up for repossession.

My roommate says, "Mail gets lost all the time." Not really, not when it's important. I know she didn't send it, but I have no proof. So, summer is coming around, and they said my car will be picked up around September. This is June. I don't know why I have to wait so long. I would owe the bank the rest of what I owed.

They said whatever the auction price is would be deducted from my current bill, making me owe nothing or a reduced price. And yes, I had to send in the papers for my 401k, but I couldn't get them in on time before they completed the repossession.

Around this time, my roommate brought me to the house of her friends, who were siblings. One was 18, another, a guy was about to turn 18, and the third, also a guy, was the same age as my roommate, 24. Their mom participated in craft shows and markets. She would craft canvas & glassware. She used to identify as a witch until her mom died, and she found God. She would talk to me about how everything has energy and how we can meditate and organize our Chakras. I will add two definitions of Chakras.

Chakras: In Indian thought, each of the centers of spiritual power in the human body is usually considered to be seven in number of energy points.

Chakra: Means "wheel" and refers to energy points in your body. They are thought to be spinning disks of energy that should stay "open" and aligned, as they correspond to bundles of nerves, major organs, and areas of our energetic body that affect our emotional and physical well-being.

Some say there are 114 different Chakras, but there are seven main Chakras that run along your spine.

"The Seven Sisters are the seven stars of the Pleiades and they correspond with the seven chakras. The Pleiades are recognized in every culture around the world, and central to the secret knowledge of ancient civilizations."

– Lyle

1.) Maia the Midwife – Root Chakra

2.) Alcyone the Queen – Belly Chakra

3.) Electra the Awakener – Solar Plexus Chakra

4.) Clean the Lover – Heart Chakra

5.) Taygeta the Storyteller – Throat Chakra

6.) Asterope the Visionary – Third Eye Chakra

7.) Merope the Priestess – Crown Chakra

Meditation: To engage in mental exercise (such as concentration on one's breathing or repetition of a mantra) for the purpose of reaching a heightened level of spiritual awareness.

The earliest documented records that mentioned meditation involved Vedantism, which is a Hindu tradition in India, around 1500 BCE. However, historians believe that meditation was practiced even earlier, as far back as 3000 BCE.

Simply follow what you believe. Do not presume anything from others, but only an idea to progress your furthered needs. Okay?

In your mind, as you read this, say, "I am kind & only harm to others is what will separate me from greater goods. The character is trying to help me with my troubles as he endured his own. The character wants you to know he is kind, too. We are all hurting, as I feel it so. He wants us to heal & find our way. Amen."

Need a break? It's okay. In the next chapter, I would like to express my ideas on what I learned through this experience. Taking a break from people's attributions that crossed my path. I will follow behind it with the duplicity of her teachings. First, I want to acknowledge thoughts on this culture and how they tie to most of the experiences we face. Those who are on a spiritual path know about Yin vs Yang.

I hope you keep an open mind and learn something from this next part. Really quick, these teachings go back in time. If you are learning something different than what you perceive, I would suggest skipping this next part. Not sure how else to inspire the unintelligent. Not everything taught in school is exact. They get it wrong just as well as a random angelic conspiracy theorist.

Oh, speaking of school, I also remember being in third grade. The teacher once asked us to create an invention. I made a pooper scooper. I took a broken end of a spatula and taped it to a 7-inch wooden four-sided stick, and I colored each side blue, green, red, and silver. Sometimes, I felt like a pooper scooper for bad people. But hey, I thought you might enjoy this little funny story about me!

PLEASE DON'T GO.

Chapter 5: The Teachings

"If the mapping system of our world has hidden islands with tribes, should note that they were dropped off there years prior to enact like they are using old technology, to stir the new aged ideals of what we're taught."

– Lyle

The day she was sharing her ideas, the day before, my roommate and I were heading to my doctor's appointment. As I was driving into town, a bird hit my car. Not even an hour after my appointment was done, we left to head back home, and another bird hit my door. Then, the next day, the lady was teaching me all of this. Her daughter, who came from another county, arrived with her Bible!

The first page I opened was this:

The Priest is to go outside the camp to examine him, and if the skin disease of the afflicted person has healed, The Priest shall order that two live clean birds, cedar wood, scarlet yarn, and hyssop be brought for the one to be cleansed. Then the Priest shall command that one of the birds be slaughtered over fresh water in a clay pot...

- Berean Standard Bible –

I figured it was all crazy or a coincidence, but it really was not. You really have to feel that connection when something happens that makes you revisit what you've seen or heard. It's like going back in time, and it feels like a revelation.

Revelations: The divine or supernatural disclosure to humans of something relating to human existence or the world.

What else have I learned? As her other daughter was giving me insight on meditation, we sat with our legs crossed and upper backs straight and put our hands together to meditate. I saw two colors, purple and blue, floating around with my eyes closed. She said not to "Say anything." Legit, these were fluid colors seen.

Blue: If you are seeing blue, it is connected to your throat chakra. This chakra often gets blocked when we do not speak our truth. It deals with people's ability to communicate and express themselves.

Purple: The third eye chakra, found between the eyebrows, is associated with purple. The third eye is important in a lot of cultures and is thought to have clairvoyance powers. It allows us to see the big picture and gain wisdom.

I am going to supply the other colors associated with the energy system as well. Since we are on this subject, we might as well express them all.

White: Seeing a white light during meditation? That is because of your crown chakra, which is found at the top of the head. This chakra is connected to source energy and is associated with our intuitions. When blocked, it can lead to anxiety, disassociation, and headaches.

Green: Green is connected to the heart chakra, which often surprises people. This chakra can become blocked from pain or trauma, but when it flows, it opens us up to give and receive love. Inner peace, forgiveness, and compassion are all associated with this chakra.

Yellow: Yellow is associated with the navel chakra. When balanced, this chakra can help you feel alive and confident. It is related to inner power and potential. If it is blocked, you may feel fearful or stagnant in life.

Orange: The sacral, or pelvic, chakra is connected to orange. As you may have guessed by the location, this chakra influences reproductive and sexual organs. It is where one's sexual and creative energy is held.

Red: Red is a color that is linked to the root chakra and is found at the base of the tailbone. As the name implies, this chakra keeps us grounded. It is what connects us to the Earth, reality, and life. When blocked, people often have issues with money, careers, food, and a general sense of belonging.

Now that you have read about the colors, and which one is each chakra (Red is 1st, and so forth), I want to now tie in OUR land founded by Native Indians. We are often told at an early age that it was rainbows and sunshine. However, the Englishmen devoured their land before setting up peace to share. Do not forget that part of history. Many of our current unaccepting Churches and powerful people deceive their own words. Certain tribes were even judged without understanding.

"Native Americans lost their history, their land, & keeping their culture alive by small Reservations & is the least talked about Genocide, as they hold a Key to our existence."

- Lyle

Lyle: *"All thee who pray; shall all be free of one."*

MEDITATION, MINDFULNESS AND SAGING

In the indigenous native Indian culture of North America, spirituality is the connection between humanity and the natural world. Nature is respected, and animals and trees are regarded as sacred entities. Animals are seen as teachers and guides in meditation. Native Americans believe that meditation is a way to transcend beyond the material world and obtain divine wisdom. Understanding the connection between humanity and the natural world is the foundation of spirituality for Native American Indians. The Native Indigenous people of North America traditionally sought the wisdom of animals and regarded them as teachers and guides. Mother Earth is an entity that is divinely sacred because all life came from her. They called the "Great Spirit" grandfather and held high regard for their ancestors. Meditation was a spiritual practice that created a way to achieve transcendence from the material world and a way to obtain divine wisdom.

Sage is a Native American ritual practiced before meditation. The Native Americans believed that it would cleanse and purify the sacred space before meditating. They would use a small bundle of sage and an eagle feather. The smoke from the sage was gently distributed with the eagle feather around the meditators, cleansing their aura.

Once things cooled down after the violence between Englishmen and Natives, many Indians were impressed by white technology. They believed that white culture must hold some spiritual power and were willing to hear what missionaries had to offer. Some became practicing Christian converts, while others violently opposed any white influence at all. For those who are upset that I used the term "white," that is what German men were, and that is what I am. We have the right to show our ancestry background just as much as everyone else.

One of the most successful efforts at Evangelization, at least by white standards, was the mission of the Cherokee Tribe in the Southeast part of our country. Presbyterian, Baptist, Moravian, and Congregationalist churches all sent missionaries to the tribe in the first two decades of the nineteenth century, and they were pleased with the response they received. Not only did the tribe convert to Christianity in large numbers, but they also chose to adopt many other aspects of the white culture that surrounded them. They constructed roads, incorporated architectural ideas, and developed a political system and a constitution.

Other tribes were dangerously conceited because they did not want their teachings to be changed and thought of other men as evil.

This perspective extends to us all. It is possible that one thinks we are evil. As the Bible suggests, evil existed before man came to earth. Is cleansing our spirit, mind, body, and soul such horrendous acts? That would show your spirit is dark within you. Need I say more? *The meaning behind all this is that we do not work together as just one person, group, or goal. We take all interests from people in all churches and members of society who provided the foundations for a robust society. (***The older lady suggested taking what I learned and then going home and finding other truths.***)* So, as I did. I investigate further vital information to shape my opinion on what I am discussing.

We covered a little bit about chakras, colors, Native Americans, and other cultures. Now, I would like to discuss the power of prayer. While praying and meditating, I grabbed the Bible afterward to pray a little more. I took my grandmother's rosary necklace, put it around my neck, and closed my eyes. I saw two more colors: Green and Pink, which both resemble your heart chakra. When you pray or meditate, as explained, it tells you to open up more of that energy point. As it was a select sign, be more loving. When I saw these two colors during meditation with my roommate's friend, whom I mentioned, my body started vibrating. This led me to meditate all the time and achieve a vibrational sensation in my body.

The blue I saw was to prove I was not talking or opening myself up more; I was remaining shy or quiet. The purple represented my strong belief that I need to follow the path to reveal more wisdom we carry within ourselves through meditation or prayer, depending on whether one chooses light or hate. I am not Baptized, nor do I follow a specific religion. I prayed for answers, and this is the knowledge I seek to understand. I don't know everything, but only what my mind allows me to see. When I mentioned the power of prayer, some might think I am crazy, but it is true. I am not mocking our higher power. I want to explain this before I tell you what I saw so we have a better belief as we follow through the advanced process of our awakening.

Our Bible has been written, re-written, etc. If there is harm or judgments placed upon it by those who are outraged or disbelievers to be placed upon, should that be something you follow? It is our job to find the tests, equations, and truths as we evolve through humanity.

We experience mind-bending breakthroughs as we surrender ourselves to the breaking point of being above in space, finding other places to support life. *(Nukes were created by Oppenheimer, as he saw visions of creating a chain reaction through the creation of the Atomic Bomb & Einstein also helped with the calculations in the 1960s to destroy Asteroids hitting our planet. They hoped that countries would not use it to destroy themselves.)* Our life form has been hidden from us. People talk about how the Bible portrays metaphor after metaphor. All the technology for aircraft and weaponry (similar to Star Wars) currently exists.

"As we travel through the galaxy with our sun & aligned planets, as our Galaxies moves by magnetic invincible force. We're on our way to the lost worlds of Andromeda Galaxy, that it too could hold secrets with others there or a fresh world to start. As If space is light, anything of space will be light, due to gravity being a natural rather than a force, like on earth. So, anything will travel of light speed."

- Lyle

"Similar to star Wars- A Force Field is a Population Protection device- That works by similar ways like a Dam. Turbines moved by water, that is connected to a Generator, then the friction goes into the Transformer that give off Electric. That goes in a indirect line of transfer, as if you were to use a Stun gun, that has 2 points with a power button, that connects the electric together. As a Dam would offer the constant flow of Electricity that makes it last longer than a button or anything in similar fashion that gives off Electric."

"We Terraformed Earth, to hold bad spirits, as the rest of the Galaxy is born to morals & faith, that exist in the other 7 worlds aligned with our Chakras, as we breed amongst the stars".

– Lyle

We are living in a simulation where what you see only with the information given must be the truth. Once you question it, they consider you to be a liar or a nutty nerd who does not know anything. Then why does science say millions of years ago when we are in 2024? **GUESS WHAT!** Remember wat I said in the beginning? I'll explain more here.

We founded this Earth 2024 years ago. Day 1 marked our independence and freedom to breathe fresh air and so forth. Really think about that for a moment. It could be true, or it could not be true. I am trying to help us understand our meaning. We had fallen angels who were prisoners in space for their wrongdoings. They were the ones who separated and set up our foundations. We have had different ethnicities from the beginning; they looked just like us. Just think, they are now finding ways to build spaceships that acquire warp holes or the theory of faster-than-light. The Space Force was created to set up war fronts to protect not only our nation's world but also from space. I say this because one night, while looking up at the sky with one of my cousins, we saw something blue/white warp that dispersed like a bright light – similar to what you might see in Star Trek's version of warping in time. I hesitate to share this for fear of being laughed at. When the power of prayer gives you revelations, the lady told me that I would have revelations after revelations. I also want to clarify that the teachings about the Bible and meditation were only told to me; everything else I've shared comes from my own understanding, not hers or anyone else. I am now stepping into a piece of the rabbit hole truth about YOU & I.

"If a leader sends his own troops out to a selfish war, ye will do the same to its own people. Ye is also referenced to a man or woman, even the other texts/scriptures you read that mention "Ye," so be cautious of both sexes that deem powers. Remember, the majority rules if 'The People' are at large to stop it & also Federal Military officials are to do their jobs of act of Treason upon such leader thereof that thinks such ways, if not? Then, it was built to go against you." -Lyle

Jesus wasn't born 2024 years ago, as he was born in the Andromeda Galaxy. He was brought here on day 1 AD. When the prisoners were dropped to scavenge around the earth to see if it would sustain life after the fallout. Of nuking the Dragons, which are now called dinosaurs, as they are evil, the Bible talks about what existed before man and the evil acts the prisoners enacted on each other, which resulted in the bad spirits that exist today. The Pope & the creators of the Vatican made up symbols that meet up with the Bible's symbols to make you "think" you're at the end of times. When it's premeditated to have you assume so, & bow down to the enemies.

As the meat eating dragons aren't the only evils that existed. Being hell realm, it was warlocks, demons and witches with angels who lost their wing as a metaphor as the nuke reference is a term for powerful magic. If any dinosaurs exist still, they're below US under the firmament. As the BIG city being built is under us, but above the firmament.

"The footprints & bones of Dragons to Dinosaurs are of 500+ years, not Millions as they would be eroded overtime by the elements."

– Lyle

"The end of time will be when our government is done with the underground big city. Those living there, already knowing or not knowing about us, they will be safe. As those at the top will be running scattered unless the world breaks apart."

– Unknown

The Delk Print, one of the most controversial evidences that Dinosaur and Human co-exist
#dinosaurs #paleontology #creationism

"By the way, here is a picture, of what was found in stone around July of 2,000 near Glen Rose Texas. Believe it or not, but they also recently found out that the current DNA structures within bones, indicate the lives of them are a lot earlier, than later. Bones contain DNA. So a blood sample is not always needed. Imagine that. God gave the fallen, beasts to eat, but may have killed off the good ones."

- Lyle

We will not find answers about our lives until something from our path of leaders can prove them to us. As we see and hear things throughout our lives, I reckon we are all aliens. I will explain: we are on an earth rock in space. We travel in space, which results in aliens, and we have had the technology of UFOs created by the Air Force. So, they can use the term "Aliens" for the government to make money from silly accusations. To use a fake UFO crashing, they might even set up the idea of aliens.

"The UFO was a man made object, to enact for business & profits off the word Alien to deceive. The MORE you know."

– Lyle

"Area 51 is all about aircraft technology,

With a potential sand door that opens, with layered levels below. If any DNA construction is to take place (cloning). The term alien is the creations below as well as us, if any is to be."

– Lyle

"The apostles grew up around Jesus, as they were his friend from birth. The apostles were ordinary men with no powers, but after Jesus's death & the powers of God's. They tried to spread the word, & thus was the end of the 12 men. As the powers were all

91

gone with no evidence, but scripture. So one of the Royal Roman churches, that started after all the spiritual battles & some Jews, killed the apostles. They didn't want secrets getting out. As they hide the scriptures, taken from the Apostles, now in the book of Demonology & Witchcraft is upon the Popes possession, that's why the King had Jews & Greeks to decipher."

- Lyle

"The 12 disciples of Jesus, in order of calling, are Simon Peter, Andrew, James (son of Zebedee), John, Philip, Bartholomew (also known as Nathanael), Matthew (also known as Levi), Thomas (also known as Didymus), James (son of Alphaeus), Thaddaeus (also known as Judas, son of James), Simon the Zealot, and Judas Iscariot.

13- As a new member as God said, "Let him be a Prophet of New Times- Lyle Light (also known as) Tommy, Son of God."

– Said Spirit to Lyle.

"Don't forget, the Roman Catholic Empire, prosecuted Christians. As they still face it today. As some don't even understand the Crimes against humanity, the Romans forced and yet proclaimed to have God's sight? God doesn't murder for the sake of Land taking. He accepts murder if you murder someone. Eye for an eye. The Roman path is of no God, but evil, after the Original Romans were taken over."

– Lyle

"After the fall of Pagan from Jerusalem to Rome, it was Roman Christian, then switched to Roman Catholic, as Christians then branched off of Catholics, with switched Scriptures, as we now call it Roman Catholic. So who destroyed and conquered who? Again, a such God doesn't destroy."

– Lyle

92

"Ice age happened years before, to freeze the evil that got sent here. Then, the Great Flood happened before 2024 years ago to sustain life from the Gods wanting to turn Hell into something else, it was also set to wipe out the bad of around 4,000+ years, but the ones that lived through the Ice Age- is what caused the big battle, now to lost powers during this timeline."

- Lyle

"The 12 disciples of Jesus, in order of calling, are Simon Peter, Andrew, James (son of Zebedee), John, Philip, Bartholomew (also known as Nathanael), Matthew (also known as Levi), Thomas (also known as Didymus), James (son of Alphaeus), Thaddaeus (also known as Judas, son of James), Simon the Zealot, and Judas Iscariot. A 13th new member as God said, "Let him be a Prophet of New Times- Lyle Light (also known as) Tommy, Son of God."

– Said Spirit to Prophet

In doubt if we were in contact, conspiracy theorists suggest if Reptilians exist, they are not actually Reptilians (they look like us). This could be a form of cannibalism due to elite forces. Our government might sacrifice a soul for technical advantages. I am not saying I believe this; I am only following the rabbit hole of sacrifices. Wouldn't you? The next insight I want to deliver is something that some may already know while others may not. Again, it's about perspective! Okay?

Understand that 2024 is when the earth was founded. Noah built an "Ark." We also had 7 "Arch" Angels that were fleets from the 1st Andromeda Galaxy and the 2nd Alpha Centauri Galaxy, which landed us here in the Milky Way Galaxy. Hence, why does the military name their fleets? Do you think it was just a snap of the fingers for our existence here? We have DNA/Lost data, which is why we fight in other countries. Not only for resources, but for lost technology information from years ago concerning what happened when we founded this planet. Just some of these countries cannot get the tools needed to carry them out etc.

This is another perspective from which to look at our lives. If you had a country, wouldn't you want to dominate so others couldn't be harmful in the future? Most people who know me call me a conspiracy theorist. When we don't take time to see the bigger picture, it is not about downplaying someone's knowledge, but about seeing what you did not see the first few times; you judge someone's thoughts. It takes the right person to finally grasp the concept. Could the ideas of Angels deceive us from the Bible? Or could the fleets be named after the real Angels? I am not mocking them; this is my understanding of how we got here… and I am trying to inform you. Angels are another word for "Spirit." Some who pass become "Angelic Spirits." Be careful of those who claim to be an angel or have seen one. Most angels will not reveal themselves to you. This is a dimensional law; they are not allowed to! I wouldn't just write this if it weren't so…

"Some Angel's are Orbs, as the one's with wings come in human form, to help those upon your path."

– Lyle

Next, this might take a swing away from the spiritual world to what the middle class exonerates in. Call me a conspiracy theorist if necessary. One thing most do not realize? Mortgages – yes, I said it. Mortgages. Mortgages are a setup scheme to get you into a "Loan Market" that you pay back. Only if you have a solid concrete ground for your house of establishment. Then, you buy insurance; in most cases, you need a solid ground to buy house insurance. Then? You can "borrow" from the bank, as in they take a mortgage out. You PAY monthly. If you stop? Guess what? They take everything. Like taxes. What crimes did we commit to gain sanctions/fines if one does not pay taxes? To whom, what crime was committed to keep paying said land taxes? I can see helping & paying the state. If we lived in a free country, we would not pay taxes on land we owned. Period. That is why you cannot get an Allodial Title.

Allodial Title means you own it, and it cannot be taken away from you, due to the fact that our free United Country is owned by the Federal Government. The "Board of Governors," which oversees banks, regulates the nation's supply growth and well-being, and sees activities from the Reserve Banks, will provide "Mortgage Insurance," which they overlook. These programs are pushed by banks, again, what they overlook. When they raise rates, it is to "calm inflation," so the more consumers have in rates, the higher the bill.

So, you're paying taxes on land that goes to the State, which the Federal Reserve looks over. The FR was created on Dec 23, 1913, to help manage assets. The government is the landlord of your land from whom you rent. Imagine that, and you thought you were free. If you don't pay taxes again, you get it taken away from you. So, learn how to save and fix your issues. Whether it's yourself, your car, or your house. I'll preach: try to live with basic needs and not judge what others do not have. Don't get a mortgage because it was set up in the early 1930s to help the States from the Great Depression – a way to help get themselves out of debt. Get a mortgage if you have a set income to supply your needs through the loan system. If you understand what I'm saying, you're paying the crime of "Living" by paying taxes on a "Free" country land that you do not own. We are free due to the men & women who have given their lives for our freedom from terror. That is your only freedom. Everything else you pay. You might own the home on a "deed," but that is another name for receipt. The land is not yours… and never will be.

"Men shouldn't tell woman what to do with their body, but if a woman wants to have the right to abort a child, instead of adoption, then it would be under rape, incest and allow 1 abortion mistake prior to the 2. As it's not the baby's mistake, a woman couldn't keep the legs closed, use protection that has been created to save lives. So, hurt the baby? Kill the baby? Shall we let the Dr do it? Or sell it to China? Then let the US get a tax kick back? Or lay back next to a volcano, and push the baby out into the fire to abort it. You killed a kid for sexual enjoyment. Bravo. As I'm pro life, you are the killer. So judge me or others to save a life? You complain to want to abort a baby, but most of you cried to free Palestine, with those young kids dying, but you Will abort your own? Pathetic. If you don't learn now. To those of any murdered sin, you won't see heaven, unless you save yourself and your own self proclaimed un-awakened mind.

To get it to be 100% yours, due to certain districts through states, you may need to pay "fees" to obtain an Allodial Title. An Allodial Title is to show and prove absolute ownership. How much do you take care of your land versus letting it go hog wild? Let that sink in. Since all land is considered eminent domain by the Federal Government, why fight it? We send ourselves to work and pay our taxes. If you had the full title of ownership, you wouldn't have to pay taxes unless someone is brave enough to challenge it. Why do you think some Senate /Congress leaders want to get rid of the Federal Reserve or change how it functions? To gain actual freedom. Once you wake up to that realization, you will understand my point of view. I hope you do. Most politicians make money off our taxes & keep supplying the poor communities with the programs that make them money. Per 7,000 average residents or more, per district of each senate /congress member looks over. So, if your community is poor, with broken roads and vague city streets, where is it all going? But again, I am just a dropout. I know nothing; this is what the lady taught me. Yes, we will say that. This is just a book of my thoughts. Oh, I like purple. It is a good color for unity.

Nevertheless, the more you know, the more you question everything! Now, back to other things, but first?

"The worst part about religions brainwashing society, is I feel bad for those that get sucked in to it. They may judge those trying to wake them up to realize, we've been lied to, to fight for your existence truth. You can just be a decent person, but that's very hard for most to do, so laws are created to align you, with the agenda of controlism, when we're meant to be free."

– Lyle

"The United Equals Country can merge into Canada to help restore its foundation. As I foresee it. & Getting rid of the Cartel of Colombian and Mexican Gov't. Up to the Panama Cana; to border south America. So all Equals can live under freedom, for those who choose it. As we connect all people and resources together."

- Lyle

PLEASE DON'T GO.

"If the Bible talks about knowing what's in space from our Apollo 8 mission to the moon and the Astronauts spoke of what they have seen- Describes the Bibles words in in the beginning of Genesis- And God said "Let there be light and there was Light" as they signed off- If someone can deliberately say in a Bible how earth was in Space? Wouldn't that be a start of realizing, I could be on to something here? As nothing else adds up to what we know currently about ourselves, but the Metaphors in the Bible. That some or all seem to miss."

– Lyle

Genesis 1:14-15 implies that the expanse which includes the sun, moon and stars and also includes other space.

Chapter 6: My Other Thoughts

"Adam & Eve are a part of the prisoners I speak of in Chapter 5. That were dropped down to earth, because they wanted to overthrow the Powers as they also committed sin as they made things worse by eating the poisoned apple they were told to eat by a snake aka a (Bad Witch) because all bad souls that were here also, on top of them, due to Earth being Hells Realm.) Adam was his brother we now call Lucifer; his wife Eve, now Lilith, as that's what the Witch wanted & waited for them because she sensed their acts, but they were defeated, & God (Joseph is God) tossed Adam & Eve to be the Guardian of Hell due to them wanting power, as they control the bad souls & God, Mary & Jesus control the Heavens Lords, which is now Yin & Yang, Magic was used & bound to be back then, but this is again the hell of bad souls. As people from the fleets scattered off into groups to start life, they had Good Light power. As they fought the big spiritual battle against the Good vs Evil. As the evil gods that existed before has been perished & powers taken away from the Good & Evil to have Peace, as those who lost power but still lived. So those couldn't learn to use it for bad. Evil took ideas, then started, Royal life, to start civilization & control the use of Powers as (Catholic & some Christian Royals agreed after a Seize Fire) They made it fiction after Jesus was the last Powerful Spiritual God, along with the death of God & Mary. Jesus was born & new he had to sacrifice himself to Hells Sins for also not us, but for his brother Lucifer & his wife Lilith due to his powers. Now, we fight demons with weapons for peace in Hells realm."

-Lyle Light

"Also for another perspective truth- Jerusalem was the place Mary gave birth to Jesus when they arrived 2024 years ago. As said previously of our arrival. Adam & Eves change to evil- They knew how to act it out. They balanced Yin & Yang. Hence, the fall of the Demon city & the rise of the Christian Light Workers Church also said in the Bible but rules out the Light Workers to hide this narrative. This is where Spiritual battles started & ended. To rid of demonic figures, now bad spirits, because this is Hells Realm. Before the end of all Magic, for the good for all. When Virgin Jesus sacrificed himself after his teachings from birth age 1 AD to age 30 AD and took three years after to defeat the bad, he died at 33. Prior to the past 30 AD years of Gods we read of fighting from the Bible to other Galaxies & his parents in the bible died before him as a teen, but his parents didn't want to be known they were of such powerful beings, to hide themselves to defeat others or they would have been killed. But it was so, they were killed. His parents knew they'd all be in charge of the 3 Heavens once they died to what they created after death with their Energy when Jesus defeated the remaining Demon Gods & Witches. As Lucifer, the brother, is in charge of the bad with his wife after the Poisoned Apple & Witch as said prior. Because he, too, knew how to control power & the bad souls thus of what he wanted. All Gods were sacrificed to souls. Lucifers job is to scare you to Jesus, or you face consequences, he may be rough, but defeat him with change! Again, Yin & Yang. 33 means: spiritual significance, guidance, and historical references with protections from Jesus."

- Lyle

"If I am wrong about this world of what was bound before, why does the Vatican have sculptures that show the fall of a Religion, (Paganism) to (Christianity). This shows, my words are so, if you see past the untold."

– Lyle

"God (Joseph) Mary & Jesus protect the 3 Heavens, the Angels/Lords protect the 7 Earth Realms, along with Jesus & his

Holy Spirit. The Realms are stacked upon each other like sheets of paper, but are spread light years apart. The Heavens are Inter-dimension's/Parallel Universe beyond our eyes reality. The 1st. Sky, 2nd Deep Space, & 3rd is beyond the Space."

– Lyle

Dinosaurs were slaughtered for a food source or are on a secured island but can potentially be below us under the firmament. Hence why men used heavy-covered armor back then. Slaying the beasts, They said men vs men. If you see bones, how can you tell what it ate? Without seeing it alive first? And we use false representations of asteroids so we do not show the way we murder everything we see. I'm thinking outside of the box with the proof right in front of me. Tell us the core is so hot so we don't adventure below. Don't that me that it is not a lie, or else we wouldn't be put in nonsense wars, as JFK warned us about. They are fighting other countries for resources and hidden information while chaos persists on our own provoked agendas. The CIA has admitted to killing our president, JFK, and the older generations deceived the conspiracy theorists. Who is laughing now that the truth has come out?

"Orchestrated events by bureaucratic leaders, are when 911 became a inside job, as not only was the rise in humanity the cause of JFK, but also him not signing on to do terror events, to cause chaos, with world order, to not just enslave us to work, but to slave our minds to not think."

- Lyle Light

"There's a plot in this country to enslave every man, woman, and child"

– JFK

"The deaths on Martin Luther King Jr. & John F Kennedy & Robert F. Kennedy Jr. were solely due to the rise of humanity getting together and the corporate greed that became after it. Of working till you die. As the era of jobs, weren't as barbaric as they are now, with policies galore & local farmers/small businesses taken out, again by corporations, as the People were lied to. As that is the conspiracy we all knew, due to what JFK said."

– Lyle

Yet I am some nutcase to what some of you think of me already. I am trying to make you aware of the unknown and how we perceive things. You really must think about it. We are born into laws that we think are normal. Some of us do not question them. The ones who do are trying to find meaning. Throughout the years, we all have been repressed, sold, and abused.

Isn't it time we found out OUR truth? I am not asking you to believe me. This is for you to take how you want. We all were slaves. Every ethnicity known to man has been put in slavery. Our country broke slavery due to our fathers finding rights within our spirit, known as the Bill of Rights/Constitution. We must now be paid for our work in compensation. We work for one another. What does slave mean today? Work for me, and I will try to reap your pay and violate your civil liberties, and you must now fight in court to prove wrongdoing. (Certain jobs I worked will prove this to be so.) Loopholes. Need I say more?

All I am asking here is to question. Question what does not make sense as well as what does. Question things you would never think about. Some of us will move on and only think about the future. I think about our past, present, and future outcomes. Can anyone tell yet? Am I a dreamer? *I ponder on the inevitable situations,* really only until I have a conclusion. If I ever end up with a heart attack, suicide, or any death that does not revolve around me reaching old age? It is probably because I put some truth in this book. We need to survive. That is the route to existence here: Survival. You are an animal/human with a purpose. Our role is to find how our knowledge is formed and to gather what we can deliver to one another.

Lyle: "May God protect me, for all I share; demons and evils shall be despaired."

Now that I have given you a set direction of what I understand, I believe certain aspects of things said in our history lead us to where we are today. The Bible covers the majority of our beginning history. The history we learn in schools? It comes from the fallen, as they described groups that went and separated, just as the Bible says. That is why I say, question everything! My opinion on the firmament? "As Below, So Above."

The metaphor is backward. There is civilization under us. Some know, but some do not realize we are up here. These individuals are more civilized and understand basic human concepts that we up here are facing. Sometimes, it is not about having the wrong answers. It is about using the answers to open the door to unknown factors. Do not construe what you do not understand as judgment, but at least conceal the idea. If NASA technology instrument Voyager can surpass the Heliosphere in 2018, that should note the firmament isn't above us as the Voyager is now lurking among the deep space to see of Alpha Centauri is our past home, as I note, that's where we came from as it's closer to us. Could the Gods we read about today be from these areas of space? Written to assume it happened in our worlds past, from the Bible we read of now? Ask yourself. I may have answered it. If you believe me.

Now, since we covered chakras, history, and my beliefs, they have similar aspects to most cultures. I would now like to express spirits. I talk about this because when I explained my confirmation of what the lady did to me, it made me question her reliance on me.

Spirits: *The conviction among many Native Americans is that there is a malignant influence associated with a dead person released at death and capable of returning to earth as an apparition. Many groups believe that spirits haunt burial grounds or return to earth to plague the living. Despite the overall fear of spirits, some tribes feel they are harmless, and some even seek their protection. The Southeastern Indians believed that everyone had a soul that lived on as a ghost after death. Ghosts were believed to have the ability to materialize so that some individuals could see them, though others could not.*

Sometimes, we question reality; sometimes, we do not. Others come across these vibrations, and others can go their path without noticing anything. When Natives understood concepts of the land and spiritual sense, they produced:

The Vision Quest: A *ceremony that has been used in various forms for thousands of years by people from all over the planet. The modern version of the Vision Quest or Wilderness Fast typically involves four days and four nights of fasting (no food) alone in the wilderness. You may see a guardian angel in human or animal form to obtain a vision of advice or protection.*

TVQ was essential to what I experienced on my path. Otherwise, why mention it? I want to draw your attention to some of the tribe's Indigenous people. Sometimes, words speak volumes.

"History is a narrative; it is a collection of stories sanctioned by the ruling power, and reinforced through words and images that suit them. That was the whole point of taking on history painting: to authorize these moments that have been swept under the rug for generations."

– Kent Monkman

"If we must die, we die defending our rights."

– Sitting Bull

"It does not require many words to speak the truth."

– Chief Joseph

"Sometimes dreams are wiser than waking."

– Black Elk

"That hand is not the color of yours, but if I prick it, the blood will flow, and I shall feel pain. The blood is of the same color as yours. God made me, and I am a Man."

– Standing Bear

"We as Aboriginal people still have to fight to prove that we are straight out plain human beings, the same as everyone else'"

– Neville Bonner

"The secret of our success is that we never, never give up."

– Wilma Mankiller

"We are what we imagine. Our very existence consists in our imagination of ourselves. Our best destiny is to imagine, at least, completely who and what, and that we are. The greatest tragedy that can befall us is to go unimagined."

- N. Scott Momaday

"We only have one earth. Let us take care of it."

– Deb Haaland

One of my favorite quotes by a world-famous singer!

"It would be wonderful when black history and native American history and Jewish history and all of U.S. history is taught from one book. Just U.S. history.

-Maya Angelou

"Be the change that you wish to see in the world."

– Mahatma Gandhi.

I mentioned Gandhi as the last quote because he is the last one I would like to address. There are a lot of people within our past, present, and soon-to-be future leaders who have a heart just as good as these individuals and me. If I had the power, I could decide between Heart and obedience.

Mohandas Karamchand Gandhi, the spiritual leader known as the "Great Soul of India" and champion of the Indian movement for independence, was assassinated on January 30, 1948, at the age of 78. Gunned down in New Delhi Durir Vigil by Hindu extremist Nathuram Godse. Gandhi's civil disobedience tactics went on to inspire civil rights leaders worldwide. After Godse realized, people would betray or hate him.

Gandhi is most famous for his philosophy of nonviolence, which has inspired civil rights leaders around the world. But his legacy is facing fresh scrutiny against modern ideas about race, feminism, and nationalism.

One aspect of the disquiet with Gandhi is his views on religious pluralism. Hindu fundamentalists do not like it —

particularly his ideas of interfaith harmony and his absolute insistence that India is [a secular state rather than a religious one] like Pakistan. [That] is not something they can easily accept. It goes contrary to their ethos. He did make some questionable investigations on his journey. He was honest about it. He did not repeat it. There is a difference... I am only trying to prove that he was prejudiced at an immature age. As he got older, he wanted everyone to be equal.

He died. He died fighting for rights, as evil had been in charge for an exceedingly long time. Everything is getting mocked, mocked in front of our faces. It hurts me so much. Do you not see it?

Now that I have covered a part of the inevitable. You can look all these up for yourself; I do not portray mistaken information. All I am doing is supplying it together to mediate the concept of a system of symbolic truths and differences. If I confused you, I am sorry. It cannot be explained any other way. Maybe a few words could be re-worded, but I like my way. Do not be afraid to foresee things you did not imagine before. I hope we learned something from what I have discussed so far. If I have not shown or given you another sense of belonging, then I failed. What makes life more important is when we wake up and realize why I am here. Need a break? In the next chapter, I will explain the night I remember.

This is a short chapter because, again, this is not about big details, as I said before; it is about perspective, again... It is not taught. I want YOU, the reader, to think, "What could have happened next." Then, use your own idea. Then, help yourself do something good out of the ordinary. I do know that our Bible is a metaphor played out for you. It may be for good or for you to not experience your true self. You do not need to believe me... but remember who said this? "Show me a man that gets rich by being a politician, and I'll show you a crook." - Our President Harry Truman!

It is hard to get people to understand the difference between the ones who are trying to wake you up for the better calling and those who are blinded by a well-managed system of narcissistic destruction and fake happy PR smiles of those who have been in charge for years and have not fixed a thing. They need to go, period! The next chapter will explain the root cause of drafting this novel...

PLEASE DON'T GO.

Chapter 7: What Happened to Me

July came around, and I started taking the older lady, who brought my attention to the energy, to her craft shows. We would have coffee and talk about life. I mean, this all started because my roommate had been doing ignorant stuff since she lived with her. She said, "She knew how she acted." I had been doing these markets for most of June. I had to drop her off at one of these events because I had an apartment. I had to get oil done on my car and a new window. My roommate locked the keys in my car, so I had to buy another window, she did not ever pay me back. Even though my car is getting repossessed (No White Sage can solve this problem.) It is fine! (Sarcasm) Her son is with me, the 18-year-old as well. I had to take him to work afterward. As I was there, the brother talked about how he was confused with himself. He brought his bowl, and the garage was near this river. So, we walked down and told me, "I'm evil." As he started smirking. I did not think anything of it. I figured he was joking when passing the bowl. He says, "Do not fall into the water. You will see death." I thought he was getting weird.

He then said, "I don't know." I say that because my brother and I were in the garage, and we put these frogs in there and watched them "blow up" in the microwave. Then he mentioned that when he was little, he would chase his sister naked and make her cry.

I said to myself, am I dealing with a psychopath, or is the entire family this demented?!

As we headed back up to the garage, I said to myself, "I hope I have enough." Ha. Nope. I was lacking $100, and the owner let me slide. He said, "Come back and give it to him someday." I was shocked to see him do that. I did go back to him two years after this… He was shocked to know I had come back. He said most people do not. Imagine the people he trusted but did not care about. What do I get out of that? If you are okay financially, or just have a heart? It is called helping. Regardless of whether you think someone will repay you or not. Always expect the unexpected. That, indeed, is something to not take for granted if it happens to you in this life.

So, anywho. I drop him off at work. I then went back to the craft show event to pick his mom up.

I go to the table next to her, it is a winery. I tried some of the wine, and it was delicious. I just happened to stand and look at there's a sign saying their next event. It said July 15th. For some odd reason, my gut sank. I felt nauseous... that was only seven days away. At the same time, I am riding in the car with her. She tried to talk to me about how much weed I had been smoking with them.

Remember, my roomy is the one who started smoking. Then she brought underage friends around 17 and 18 years old, and then the older brother she dated. The mother told me and wanted me to stop smoking. So... I do. On the night of July 15th, 2018, my roommate came home from the day shift. She says we are going over to the friend's house. Should we label them crazy people? Or is that judgmental? I am happy to say I felt saner than ever being around this energy. I am starting to question.

We eat dinner; I hear a "nock." At the door. It was the neighbor. She wanted to come smoke.

**Let us take another moment to realize something. Adult peer pressure happens in the real world, but we do not ever accept it. When kids get in trouble, knowing it was one person who did the bad, they all get punished. Adult? You. YOU get punished. Our actions make choices. It is others who influence the ones in bad directions that do not need this planet, nor rapists, nor murderers, nor fornicators, nor abusers, and nor anyone who deceives another for sharper gain if the soul partner feels diminished from being poor. They are an abomination from our Lord. - Thee who denies this is a deceiver of our higher power. Period.

So, she wanted to smoke, and I had not smoked in a week. I expressed that I did not want to. She and my roommate said, "You are a baby." You are going to listen to some older lady. (I did tell her, the older lady, some honest things; most of the things I mentioned I did wrong.)

I then took a hit. My body felt very weird, shaking, chest was pounding. and I opened the freezer door, thinking I could calm down. The neighbor goes to her apartment and comes back with a blue pill, Adderall. She said it was an Advil! Then said, "Oops." I gave you Adderall. I put it in my PM bottle. "WTF!?!?" Went through my head.

I told her to leave, and for some reason, I was okay. The feeling of pounding all over went away. My roommate and I then got ready to leave to go to her friends, as she was the one bringing the weed into their home. We stopped at a store; she grabbed a soda, and so did I. On the way there, I saw a cross in the shape of a cloud. I felt numb, not a good or bad feeling.

We leave, then pull up to the house. We go out, and I see the kids outside. The older brother had kids. They were next to the landlord in this shed outback. He told me he was cleaning the shed. I looked to see the inside. It was all empty, with nothing around or in it. I noticed that, thinking he could fool me. Knowing the shed is an entranceway to the cellar under the house. I saw the latch, which I think was a latch.

My roommate and I walked into the house. There is a door on one side, that looked nailed shut that went to the basement. Another door at the other end of the house. My friend said she thought it was a closet when she stayed here because I asked if it was the "bathroom." To get a reply of what room it is.

*Sometimes, you must look at all trivial positions of your surroundings… I mean it. You may not ever know who you're around… I went into survival mode. *

I accidentally left my drink downstairs; we went up into her friend's daughter's room. My roommate and her friend are talking about smoking; it is around 10 pm now. I did not want to because I said I smoked earlier and should cool off. I then noted I had to go down and get my drink. The roommate persisted. It was next to me. We bought the same drink. I knew I had more in my drink. I go down to get it. I came back up; they had a bowl already packed. They handed it to me, and I took it out of context, not realizing it. As I take a hit, I start to feel jolting all around me. I touched my friend, and her skin was vibrating. She said, get your mom to the other girl. The spiritual lady comes up and then tells me to come here.

I was thinking about jumping out the window. But said it aloud and noted am I going to drown?

I went downstairs, and the mom said, "Come here now." My roommate stood there in the other room. The daughter put on this religious song and lit white sage. The mom said, "Are you ready?" The daughter replied, "But brother is sleeping." The mom replied, "That's how the transition is supposed to work." I saw my friend go back upstairs while they told me to "close my eyes." I did not listen.

They put both their hands around me, placing me backward against the counter. I looked up, and I saw two dark orbs come out of my body, darting into the ceiling. My brain thought I was going a mile a minute.

Did I step into a cult family? That used me liking the energy talk to do this to me? That is what I was thinking. I called my sister, and she said I did not make sense when I snuck inside the bathroom to hide. Her GF suggested exactly what I thought. "Cult." She said get out of there if I can. But my roommate left me there. Then my phone died… I did not know what to do. Before it all happened, my friend said about the two doors I saw. I should not have looked down and seen they were nailed shut.

When I came out of the bathroom, no one heard me. (Hopefully,) I felt like someone was coming. One of their friends had come by. I "sensed" him coming. I said, "Jay?" Out loud, weirdly. He showed up with the girl's boyfriend, who was the drug dealer I mentioned earlier!?! They went upstairs, and the mother said not to cross these lines of salt she put down towards me.

I started going crazy. I ran out the door, going to the neighbor's house and no one was awake. I then went to the end of the road; there was a red house. The porch light was on, and so was the inside kitchen where the door faced you could see. (I do not know why) but I opened the door. A radio was in the middle of the stove. It was playing "Eye of the Tiger." I froze. I ran across the yard behind this tree.

I could see the daughter; she and her bf, plus his friend, got in the Drug Dealer's car, drove to the house I went to, and went inside to turn it all off. **How did they know I was there?** I saw the mom through the window on her phone as I was looking back at the house of horror. I then saw their dad go out towards the garage. I then go ahead to go to this one house nearby. The woman that lives there came out. She gave me a choice when I explained what happened to me. I said, "My name, birth date, and situation." "A lady had her daughter drugged me to do an exorcism." I gave her the fake names of the people. I was afraid too. Thinking they would know. **The feeling I felt?** like something was pressuring me. An invisible force. This force tried to radiate my head with these thoughts of violence as I did not reciprocate or dwell on these harmful actions. My spirit knew they were wrong. A random thought goes into my head. "I'll take care of you and your baby." She said, go hide in the woods. I was thinking to myself. Does she know these people too? I snapped out of it and said, "Can you help me"? She gave me her home phone and said I could call 911 or go back to where I came from to whatever house. I could not use my phone; it was dead. I asked if she could charge it for me. She did not have a charger. I was afraid to call 911.

I ended up going back to the house. I ran next door to this guy's house;* Long story short* he was a known drug dealer, as my roommate told me. So, I asked if I could use his phone because

112

he was outside smoking a cig. (It was nice out.) He let me take a drag off his cigarette. (I do not smoke those.) I had to then, I was getting anxious and tired of this bull crap) I felt numbness on my lips like he put something on it. Then told me, "My phone died, sorry bro."

The daughter, bf, and friend come back... she tells me, the daughter, "Where have I been." They thought I went down by the water, due to me stating I was going to "jump in the river." Obviously, I did not. * I had this weird, numb feeling they wanted to kill me and drain me in the river. *

The mom then took me. She told me to lay on the floor and took her sage and Music again, but I was on the floor. When - the mother was trying to finish her voodoo? My hair looked like I got electrocuted. Legit... I then figured my roommate had left, taking my car. Her excuse the next day? She had to work. So, as I am sitting in the daughter's room... She is lying down with her bf, asks me to leave, locks her door, and puts a book in front of my face with a little girl on it. She said to her bf that she is tired of seeing her while crying heavily. He says, "Who"? I then hear her brother's door "lock."

The mom was downstairs sitting in a chair (back straight up, legs crossed). I went into the bathroom. I noticed her going into her room. She locks the door. I then went ahead to grab water out of the fridge, I did have a bag with me. I carry a bag with me with clothes and supplies for any reason. (Mainly if the car breaks down.) But this is a soul breakdown instead. Also, I did not even have my car. The roomie took it! I need to start not being so nice! I start walking outside, I sit in the yard. I felt weird, like anxious. I kept thinking about their father and how he got up and left to the back of the house last night. Cause when I saw the daughter, when she asked me where I was when I was hitting the cigarette. I said, "Where did your dad go?" GUESS what she said? "You did not see anything. "

So, as that is playing in my head, these people are playing me! I started to get up and just go for a walk. I went around this one house. A guy was outside. I asked him if I could use his phone. He said, "Sure."

But the guy did not come back out... he judged me. How dare he?

I just said, "screw it." I went down this path, where a trail was. A house nearby had these dogs outside. They started barking badly. Like they saw a ghost. I then saw this army guy with a backpack coming out of the trail. I knew he was in the army, because of the backpack. I decided to change my clothes after he left. On the trail, lol.

As I am coming back, my older brother is coming back to the house on his motorcycle with a trooper behind him. And my parents are coming from the opposite road because the mother called them.

My parents' side of the story? They are demanding, "Where is my son?" That is not the case. They see me walking down the road. It has been about an hour since I was gone. They sit me down in the kitchen.

The mother says, "Do you know the name you called me last night?" I say, "No." She replies, "You will." Oddly, I mentioned that I felt like I took away the mischievous spirit on my walk.

The daughter turned and tried to hand me a sticky note with the lady's number on it. The one I went to and said, "I'll take care of you." She then took it back away. I wanted to know what happened to me. The mom spoke up and said, "Go to the hospital before it's too late."

I did not go. They told me to not ever say anything about what happened, or I would be disappointed in the outcome. Why would you? So, they gain power from you? The daughter spoke up and said to my mom, "It wasn't supposed to make me go crazy like that." At the time, my parents took me back home. I do not want to step inside for some reason, not even in my parents' home. My mom called my sister and told her. My sister calmed me down.

**The only time I felt like my sister was against me was when the girls made fun of me for being gay. Doing the fake page, etc.? If you flashback to me talking about school. The one friend that had a sister who would buy us drinks at 14? I stayed with her. A week. She got drugged up and tried to fight me. She came at me while I took her hands and locked them down. So she could not hurt me. I did not punch her. Nor hurt her. Blocked her from hurting me. She was on the phone with my sister because they knew each other. My sister knew she was a drug addict liar. The woman yelled and screamed.

My sister said I had anger issues. When in reality... she did not believe me. Made an excuse and said, "My eyes were black." When I yelled at her for not believing me, I had bad judgment for my sister for a while. Her ability to not believe me. Could result in why I treat her like I do today. Her lack of judgment caused her own experiences of why I turned out to be a butthole. Any who...

I get myself back to normal again. My roommate picks me up at my parents', but my dad says, "Be careful; there might be someone in your closet."

When I got back to the apartment, I found this dollar store bag with a shirt in it. It said, "The buck stops here."

I thought it was directed towards me because it felt like it. Or else why would it be on my table?

My roommate was quiet. She had her mom come over; cause afterward, she told me not to eat anything. Her mom was bringing lasagna. Ok... her mom comes, and we eat, etc. My roommate gets in the shower. Again, I do not smoke cigarettes... but her mom offered me one. I mean, after everything that has happened. Wouldn't you? I told her what happened. She said it happened for a reason, but my daughter is "using you." You need to get away from her. I try to figure it all out, but nothing.

So, as the night went on, the roommate had this military guy come over. Long story short? He came back, saying she gave him something. Something she did not disclose, so she got mad I talked to him about it.

I remembered her telling me her other ex gave her something. I got checked before we moved into our apartment at Planned Parenthood. When I was in the room with the nurse? It was all hot inside, like I was warming the room with my presence as it was around 65° outside and sunny. They had the air conditioning on, so I wondered with the weather being all crazy, if I was the reason for it? The test came back negative. I reassured myself. My roommate was the only chick I dabbled with. Only once. When her and I do it? It felt like pressure was surrounding me to do so, like an invincible force pushing me. So, I said to myself, should I get another test? I did. Her cousin just happened to stop by when I did. She even looked at it. It was negative.

Sometimes, you must make sure your health matters! I do not think my roommate does. She even told me she had "gray clouds" over her head. So, it is like she knew but did not care. I guess the military guy she messed with? He was involved in skimming ATM machines and disputing fake $100 bills. I told her I did not want to see him back. (Some persons of the oath that protect us are not true or patriots if you deceive your community.) We have this local community online page that shows the delinquents. He was on it for "Have you seen this person?" A month goes by, and the roommate tells me one night we are having a heart-to-heart due to me expressing how I feel like I will always be single. She then said, "The person who will be in my life will be in yours. "Just he will not always be there she noted. What does that mean? Then kicks my dog. Oh, I wanted to lay her down and make pain on her. But I held in my negative emotions!

The next morning goes by; I wake up, go pee, and head back into bed. I feel this "jolting "again. I see black and white flames beside me in a walkway-type manner. I look up and see a bright Golden S. *This was a good feeling* As the black and white flames represent Yin and Yang.

I open my eyes and close them again. I see myself looking back down at myself. There is this long black arm coming across my bed. Then I woke up. *That one made me feel off. I did not know what it meant. What do you think? Break time? We are going to take the next chapter and explain who I met. Did the "S" resemble Sacrifice, Survivor, or being Saved? Or all 3? I feel like a Saved Survivor, Sacrificing my thoughts to have you understand me, or you can laugh and judge. Though, who am I kidding? I write in this diary Memoir like anyone will understand me, especially when I talk about our existence. After it all, I didn't want to exist anymore. I wanted to depart this earth. I KNEW I was stronger than that. If I wasn't here? I would not be sharing my story. Maybe one time, I did want to do something stupid. Almost did. Till I heard someone coming and saw a little Gecko on the ground that needed help getting across the little path onto the next side, helping that little creature was the boost I needed to stay alive. This was around a time I'd like to not say. Doesn't matter now; we have become better from our dark past as God is my Light. The little things add up. The "Attention to Detail" of your environment. If you've helped any creature, why not help a human? I didn't know if that Gecko was a bad little Gecko or a good little orange critter. I just helped it. I know others think the same as me… Just hope to find a like-minded someday. It's okay to be by yourself sometimes. If I haven't shown that? You will understand after the rest.

PLEASE DON'T GO.

Chapter 8: Aug 28th

For a while now, my roommate has said she was talking to someone. I had no idea. She then asked if we could pick up someone. I said sure. But guess what? I do not have my car. It is gone.

We picked this military guy up, but we had to use the neighbor to pick him up. I sat in the back. So did the guy. When we got back, I told him I planned to leave. Before I say that? I told him I saw myself working in an Auto care facility of some type because we were talking about my different jobs etc. When the roommate went into the bathroom, he asked, "Why?" I planned to leave. I told him exactly what happened about the July 15th occurrence. He then tells my roommate that I told him, when she walked out and they went inside her room. She then got upset cause she texted me, saying, "Why did I tell him?". I'm trying to help us "both." As she didn't explain further. She just walked away.

Time goes by, and he is now staying with us. They have left me alone a couple of times while they went and goofed off doing other drugs that I did not want to do. How do I know? *She has needle pricks on her arm, and her nose looked red as did he* - (if it was not for _some_, not all, military members abusing the system of drugs, or the Army giving it to the soldiers to stay up longer in battle. It would be much safer.)

More time passes, and the military guy tells me he feels her "bad" vibes. I tell him to be careful. Do not get weirded out when I say this: "I think she may harm you." He gets scared and tells me he talked to his dad, but he told her the roommate. Again, she is upset.

*I felt deep down, she would do something to him." - If she knew I liked him. Because he and the roommate went with me one day the following month to my aunt's funeral, as my family was fighting to get my aunt's ashes back to put her next to the rest of

118

the family. My uncle strayed himself from everyone when we wanted to pursue her wishes of being buried." * - the one that treated me with kindness- Any-who, I mean, her bf was decent looking. He reminded me of my grandmother in many ways. After we get back from the funeral...

The neighbor came by wanting me to babysit her kids while she and my roommate got more weed to restock. Something said "ask" the little girl. I asked her, "Does mommy and my friend like me?" she said, "No." She is about to be 5. I said something to my roommate, and of course, she would deny it. But the neighbor told her daughter to not say those things… why? Cause there true?

Her new boy toy was trying to establish me as a friend, but I had too much going on for what they did to me. My friend spoke up and told me my "mom" wanted her to turn me straight. (My mom denies it) even though she told me to not come back home if I liked guys." Around my teenage years. That stays with you forever. Yet my mother lies to my face. Some parents are unintelligent power-hungry sickos. Thinking about what they think or say matters after not showing respect towards YOUR child.

Respect your parents. Do not respect them if they start treating you like you do not feel comfortable. That is putting the power of the narcissists in their place. Parents should be loving; they give life and should accept what they have made.

*Bad parents who deceive their children shall be an abomination to our higher powers. *

More time goes by, and the roommate's brother is now involved. She is having him stay with us. He would say to me, "God hates fags." On a repeated basis. Only when her bf was not there he would always ask where his big knife was, as he suggested one night; he liked to watch us sleep. He noted he killed his family pet one time, started laughing and said, "I'm just fibbing you." He spoke. Acting like a psychopath. *Yet these people have the audacity to call me crazy!?!*

119

Then, later that night, I tried to tell the new boyfriend about him and more of her, when everyone was asleep. As he suggested, when I was getting help? Because he didn't believe me for what they put me through.

The new boyfriend also suggested when I was "getting help?" because he did not believe me for what she put me through. He said he and his friends thought I was too nice, and the roommate did not ever hurt you. I tossed my stuff in my room, going nuts. When you know what happened!!!!

Then, the night after, he said that. He is in the room with her, and she blocks me randomly on FB. When I was trying to message her. It said it was blocked on the messenger. She said, "No, I didn't." As her bf was walking to the door to leave for work. I punched a hole in the wall. Cause I got tired of the abuse. (I bought the stuff to fix it) that is beside the point. – it looks like a new wall, though. What have I gathered? She wanted me out so she could prevail over her mistakes. Because she said, "I wish you would have hit me." The apartment was in my name! They could have left. But nope… we decided to move to the Apartments next door. Same landlord. Long story short?

I took the roomie's boy toy to work one morning, and the car jerked over, hitting two cars. It felt like someone was taking over the car. It was at least 10,000 for damages. Have not heard anything from it… They all tried to turn me into a monster and would call me a "square" because why? I did not want to do harder drugs. Be a part of the scene? With the built-in anger… I needed out before I did do something stupid. **Square means-** someone, someone who is a boring person. One that does not like new and exciting ideas.

I thought I had feelings for her bf. but I thought he was an investigator. Trying to catch me? But I figured my friend was setting me up. After I started thinking about everything, her bf told me he had to jump through hoops to just get to her. Roommate and her brother had a very weird relationship with her bf. I knew what they were doing. Yet people still think I am stupid. I told the roommate's boyfriend's mom about it all. She said, "Time will tell." I did not know what to do. Her bf told me, we will not have the same relationship as him and her with his friends. I told him we would not have a relationship at all. Why be with someone if they do not trust you? Do not ever be with a person who downgrades you or does not trust you. Period.

I took everything when I decided to finally get away from them. They were left with an empty apartment. I brought and bought 95% of all household items in that apartment. She, her brother, and her boy toy are straight-up users. Fake, prude and unintelligent! If you ask, what else made me leave? It was the fact she had me take one of her grandparents' rings one time to sell while she was at work. He found the ring and got it back. So, she got $20 selling her gramp ring. Blames me? As a setup. Wouldn't that be a sign to run? Get away? I think so.

Since I left, this entire time, I have worked at Walmart. I am there, standing at one of the checkouts, and there is this tall mom walking with her daughter. I heard the daughter, who was about 14. Say something, whispering to her mom, looking back at me. Her mom said, "That's the one going through_____." And I could not help but go, "Huh?" Went through my mind. Could there be people out here who know more about others than what we know for ourselves? I thought... I mean, to bring a "movie" into perspective? "Incredibles." However, I think in the 2nd one, they say people with superpowers are on a Govt law, saying they cannot intervene when chaos arises. To play out "Natural Events." That is my "assumption." Call me crazy, but there is a lot of truth in front of our faces that some are too blind not to see. It hurts me so much.

Later that day, I met this lady, "Dawn," who was in a riding chair at Walmart. She is someone that most people would judge. Not me. We became friends there, and she is someone who I talk to daily. Even after not working there anymore. Just a heads up? I will mention a dream I had that involved this lady. Before I did, I used to feed her at work if she was hungry, or I would give her rides home. At the same time, I was headed over to her house one time, to bring her some marinated chicken and hamburger she likes. She said she had friends over the night before. I had this dream of being over at her house, and a water gun showed up. Did not think anything of it. Guess what? I show up, and there the water gun sits. On her cooker the same way in the dream. And that was my first time being there. After all this. My ex-roommate? She tried to call the store and try to get me fired. So, on a social page... I videoed and called everything out. Wishing she would dispose of herself... because I was getting upset. Her brother's ex came to me. As I put her on recording, telling me my roommate was honest about drugging me on multiple occasions. I am HEATED after fighting to get her to talk about what happened that night, July 15th. This entire time, I have been fighting in my head and what she did to me/tried to do. As her mother told me, she was using me. (I did not think anything of it).

As I have left her my apt. Gave her all rights. Before I left? I popped her tire on her car. I judged myself. You can judge me too. It felt great to do! I realized her bf was just trying to get me out too. Because no one took the time to ever ask me, "Are you okay." All they did was belittle me in my own home. After a while, people at work knew what happened, and a lady got caught stealing, and I confronted her. She called me a "faggot." And I lost it. I said screw this place. Seems to me, wherever I go. I am getting belittled! I was told my ex-roommate called again that day to get me fired. I was tired of the bull crap. Ya know? I wanted them all 12 feet buried underground with her family, brother, herself, including her now husband and his family, too, along with the drug dealer addicts who she got the drugs from... The SCUM ex-roommate and her ignorant bf got married after I left. I found out she also invited her brother to their drug-invested honeymoon. Need I say more?

Authorities did get involved with my roommate as it has been five years so far. One of her husband's friends tried to give me this story that he was "investigating" her. And tried to coax me over there. I told the trooper I saw you there. Cause I went there to go pee inside my ex-roommate's now husband's old Camaro. (Obviously, I did not tell the police officer that.) Why? One time, the bf mentioned how he peed on his superior's desk. "What you do to others comes back at you." That is the way I see it! I could chat more about him. I would rather not make it more painful than what they already caused me. Cause after I left, he mumbled, "I'll be back." To deceive me of high hopes. A year goes by after not being there. I messaged the one lady who did that wacky stuff on me. I asked if she wanted to "burn now or after New Year's." Let us just say that almost landed me in trouble. LOL. It did - honesty is the best policy, right? I got arrested and charged with "Harassment." I paid $200. Guess what? <u>It did not hurt me.</u>

After a while, the ex-neighbor got ahold of me, the one that was at the apt. She wanted to give me back a Tupperware of mine. It was my mom's. So yes, I would like it back! Guess the roommate sneaked it on me and hid it or gave it to her, but she knew it was mine. That I give her respect for. I go over to pick it up at her mom's, who is nearby. As I walk in, I sit down. I expressed to her mom and her why I left the apt. Her mom spoke up and said, "Someone died in this apt." I was like "huh"? Come again…please? She said when she walked around the corner. She feels him. I continue to walk in the direction, and I feel this strange vibration in the hallway. We chatted a few more. I grabbed the dish and left, and that was really the last time I associated with them. First time meeting her mom, though. She seems nice. Her mom's apt was kept clean. I'm not sure why the neighbor would have hers look so nasty. She did tell me she had a miscarriage, and she had been dealing with that ever since. I then understood why once she told me. She expressed that she was outside smoking a cigarette before I grabbed the Tupperware. Do not judge everybody because you do not know their pain. Though she still fed me the wrong pill, remember? You can always forgive, but not FORGET.

I am in the car; I start blaring the music and stopping in a parking lot, singing at a random couple standing there. I then did it to someone I knew! She did not know me. She was a cashier at a store. Just knew her by going in randomly at times. Yes, they thought I was nuts. With everything going on… I had to act out in a positive way! Would you rather me be negative? I know some who would say yes, but I think… no! Now, let us take a break. Use this next small chapter and recap the moments I described, to get a better outlook. Shall we? To clear up any confusion...

PLEASE DON'T GO.

Key signs of a cult are isolating members from the outside world, controlling relationships within the cult (i.e., the leader has the final say on relationships with family and friends), engulfment within the cult, and, usually, shunning of those who leave unless they stay useful in some way.

Chapter 9: Recap and Reiki

"This is our timeline here. 2024 years ago, Gods finding earth, to defeat evil entities & the beasts, (some good dinos saved or for food source), powers sacrificed, as bad to good spirits to souls, as reincarnation supply's within, Stone age, battles, to Royals, Ministries, Cowboy & Indian battles, due to the off spread of others, sticking to their own culture, then Military battles to now Exorcism battles & Hidden Information battles, Growing Society without knowledge of power, to technology battles, of hidden scripts, to local businesses, now to corporate and control to here of Modern day life, happened between these 2,000 years, now we have modern day wars of control, hells realm as I say."

– Lyle

In this chapter, I give you explanations of my perceptions of events so that you may see, read, and feel the emotions that I intend to share with you. This is another short chapter, but I want to get us to see the revelations and aspirations followed by the deceived, as well as an understanding of Reiki, as it ties into chakras and energy. I bring up "Movies" or "Shows" (Remember in the beginning with my slogan?). "Heal the soul and open the mind together; what shall we find?"

Here are some examples of shows and movies that display the chakras, reiki, and energy.

The Grinch was a green 'monster,' and in one scene, his heart is shown beating out of his chest. This was to show the 'heart chakra.' Green often represents envy, and he is depicted as an antisocial being and he was mean to the community. However, once he was loved and made to feel welcomed, he understood the burdens of others. After this, what they thought was a dangerous creature that was seen as evil because of the color of his fur was *no longer judged or mocked. In the end, we see that all he wanted was love. ***

The scenes depicted in The Wizard of Oz are similar to an "Out of Body Experiences." Why do I say that? Did you watch the movie? Once you do, you will understand why I said it. *

The story of Shrek also resembles the principles of the "Heart" chakra. His swamp lifestyle and green-muscled body was one that was feared and avoided. Guess what? That scary monster was not his true self. He saved the Kingdom...*

This is why I acknowledge media such as shows and movies. If this is an older adult reading, this is to establish your childhood; it had to have brought some type of memory.

"When the Gov't creates a budget for film/entertainment, the sole purpose is to distract you to hide truth to our own accord."

- Lyle

We are lacking Heart. If the community had loved the two green goblins before, Shrek would not have saved the Kingdom, and The Grinch would not have found ignorance in the Governor/Corruption. Everything happens for a reason. I shall preach that, oh must I indeed so, please understand that.

I did go to a Reiki "Master," who expressed that what happened to me was for a reason. Like what my friend's mother told me. My question is, "Why?" What makes me special so that I have protection? Am I the chosen one?

"Reiki" means - "mysterious atmosphere, miraculous sign." It comes from the Japanese words "rei," meaning universal, and "ki," meaning life energy. Reiki is a type of energy healing. According to practitioners, energy can stagnate in the body where there has been physical injury or even emotional pain. In time, these energy blocks can cause illness.

126

What happens in a Reiki session?

Practitioners typically give Reiki treatment in a peaceful, secluded setting, but it can take place anywhere. During a session, the client sits in a comfortable chair or lies on a table, fully clothed.

The practitioner will then place their hands lightly on or over specific areas of the client's head, limbs, and torso. They will typically keep their hands in these positions for 3–10 minutes. If there is a particular injury, such as a burn, the practitioner will hold their hands just above the wound.

Advocates state that while the practitioner holds their hands lightly on or over the body, an energy transfer takes place. During this time, the practitioner may report that their hands feel warm or are tingling. They will hold each hand position until they sense that the energy has stopped flowing. When the practitioner feels that the heat, or energy, in their hands, has gone, they will remove their hands and place them over a different body area.

Some Reiki techniques:

The techniques that Reiki involves have names such as:

- centering
- clearing
- beaming
- extracting harmful energies
- infusing
- smoothing and raking the aura

Some Reiki practitioners use crystals and chakra healing wands to enable healing or protect a home from negative energy. I mentioned this not only because I am ordained, but it also helped me get to what you are reading today.

Lyle —*Do not fool yourself. Overnight succession does not happen. It is the journey that chooses your destination.

Recapping The Chapters: In the beginning, I mentioned I had a couple of traumatic events, plus issues with family members, as well as work situations, on top of getting drugged and put in a spot against my will. Oh, and got belittled. Did you pick up any moments and how they deceived me?

Other Revelations are:

Out-of-body experiences and helping those unexpectedly. Fixing what wrongs you have done when you realize it and have time. Meditating and seeing the colors. Thinking of out-of-the-box solutions to fix our broken. Then, seeing answers for what you thought was blocking you. Seeing a way to go out on your path within dreams or "insights." Seeing the vision and dream of everyone hurting.

Amid the overwhelming flood of emotions, with cross-shaped clouds looming and more on the horizon, I had a vision of the "Golden S." I admit that I made some mistakes. For instance, I took $100 from the Kilp, where I worked. You might wonder if I made it right. Yes, I did. After returning home, I went back, gave the money back, and was honest about what I'd done. He simply replied, "It was good to see you." As I mentioned from the start, we all have time to correct our flawed habits or mistakes. Doing so brings relief, self-discipline, and respect—qualities tied to accountability, which many of us lack. It's like when you think of someone and then unexpectedly run into them. That moment is meant to happen.

Now, to lighten the mood, let me share a humorous foodie joke I picked up while working in the restaurant industry. Feel free to take a break here, and if you've heard it before, share it with someone else!

"Why did the Hen lay her eggs?"

So, she could be dunked in her own children...

Ever think of it that way? A little dark humor for you. Don't judge me; it puts an entirely different view on "Chicken Egg Rolls." Lol... Sorry for the vegan lovers...

"Why did the Tofu cross the road?"

To prove that he wasn't CHICKEN!

Okay... Let's carry on lol sorry, I have been contemplating whether to add them to this book. So, obviously, I did. It made me chuckle.

"How can you tell if someone is vegan?"

Don't worry, they'll end up telling you...

OK, I'll stop lol working in the Food Industry; you'll gather a sense of humor quickly; if not, do not join the food industry... I mean, you need a sense of humor in most jobs and in life anyway. If you are too stuck up or egotistical about things, you're missing the laid-back fun times with others who are just trying to enjoy what they have. Humor is what also sets us off to become less depressed from a current thought or bad moment we're in. So, crack jokes, laugh, and enjoy yourself or others' company. Be positive-minded! I say this because of what I'm about to reveal... I'm still curious about this vision of the Golden S.

*** *Before we move on* ***

I didn't mention this earlier because, like everyone, I'm not perfect. A Spirit once urged me to connect with it as I wrote in my diary. I came to understand this more deeply when I discovered my roommate was drugging me. Back when I worked at Gas Trac, I had put my best friend/roommate on my health insurance plan, thinking if something happened to me, she'd receive $25,000. That's what she thought too. Hence, why drug me and tell me I'd end up dead one night we had a disagreement as it finally clicked to me, or was it the spirit telling me? I'll leave that up to you to decide.

It's crucial to know who you're dealing with and how they see you. Are you a friend or just bait for a scheme? Be mindful of what you share with others. The next time you see a shiny gold coin, fill up your gas tank, or hear about a theft or drug bust on the news, remember the dark, hidden connections that tie these things together. And no matter what, keep a sense of humor in the face of life's absurdities.

If we were to have glacier issues in the future of maybe 76+ years from now: This is my summary:

Rise in oceans to beaches tides, as we have to build up. If icebergs melt within the warmer currents, which is the case.

To effectively stop icebergs from melting, the focus should be on reducing global warming by lowering carbon emissions, which means transitioning to renewable energy sources, improving energy efficiency, and reducing deforestation; as the primary cause of iceberg melting is rising global temperatures due to climate change.

Potential, but highly complex and experimental, methods to directly slow iceberg melting include:

Above or Underwater barriers.

Building underwater walls or curtains to block warmer ocean currents from reaching the icebergs.

Ice creation from Artificial:

Collecting melted glacial water, desalinating it, and refreezing it into new ice masses to replenish the glaciers.

Glacier "blankets":

Covering glaciers with materials that are reflective to reduce solar absorption.

Pumping cold water from deeper ocean layers to the base of glaciers to cool them down.

Important points to remember:

Climate change is the main culprit:

The most effective way to stop icebergs from melting is to address the root cause – climate change – by reducing greenhouse gas emissions.

Large-scale solutions needed:

Any direct intervention to slow iceberg melting would require massive technological advancements and international cooperation. The more we know.

"Also reader, remember as hell ventures more throughout thy lands, it's up to us, to those who follow Faith, to slowly shell light unto thy darkness. Most Leaders are doing the best, with good intentions with a world full of species. Or else, you'd be dead by now, not reading this. Wars are ongoing for resources, hidden information and things you couldn't imagine so. To defeat thy enemy, is to find it's weak spot, understand numbers from ground to sky. Recourse you're steps to all surroundings with your tech against thy others, as action takes place with Hope to save as many lives as ye possibly can. If Peace is no longer of service or wanted. Be the service. Don't forget about the ones who pass, remember they fought for you. Forget thy troubles of whom that have bothered you, if you don't have evidence, not hearsay. People don't defend what's right. Only to whom they like.

If you do have proof, bring upon it & then forgive, to embrace the Wings, as you love along the way. Your death shall prosper to the Heavens to those of Light I speak."

- Lyle Light

"If we follow a Christian faithed Bible, why do all roads lead back to Rome? Which isn't of Christian faith, after Catholics took scriptures. I will bring you home if you trust me."

– The Guardian of Truth

PLEASE DON'T GO.

Chapter 10: Back In NY

Around this time, I figured, what if I went back to work at the hotel where I first worked? I'm back living with my parents, and it's giving them a headache—especially my dad. We never get along. But I need to find a job to keep myself busy and give myself a purpose.

I went to Waive-Edge Hotel, and the new FD manager hired me on the spot. I thought, "Hmm, that was easy." You know, checking in guests, checking out guests, making reservations, etc.—it's the typical stuff. I generally have a good relationship with most people, but the lady they had doing the financial part of the hotel? She didn't like me. Turns out, she was best friends with my ex-roommate's mother. Imagine that—small world, right?

As days went by, we talked about the situation because she thought we were still friends. I told her we weren't, but she didn't want to hear it. My roommate had mentioned before that people would believe her because she was a girl. So, she was saying that being a girl, she'd be more believed. Sounds like sexism to me— what about you? Some women are in prison just like some men are, so she can't fool those who aren't fooled.

Anyway, the lady at work told me a guy had died in one of the rooms before I got there. He was a millionaire. She said the paramedics found that he had overdosed on drugs. Apparently, he always had money on him and would give women free drinks at the bar.

The entire time she was telling me this, I kept thinking that someone must have done it. The front desk manager had a girl helping, and they were both friends. The woman started laughing about it because she was nearby, hearing the story and expressing her views. My gut felt an unbelievably dreadful sense, but I couldn't prove anything. Who laughs over a death?

Then, one night, while I was working, I happened to find something on the computer. I was just typing the owner's name—he has a Doctorate degree—so I wanted to see if he was well-known. I found out that the owner of the place where I'm working is known for cooking pills. That night, while I was working, I heard the GM ask, "How can I get $12,000 to fix this leak?" Then one of the workers, who was the supervisor, was using this big scale to weigh packages and determine postage costs. I jokingly asked him, "Wouldn't they use that for drugs?" I was being straightforward. He put his head down and didn't deny it!

He and I went to do rounds, checking the hotel because it was dead. The GM was in his office drinking (on the clock), and I heard him snorting.

Note that my intuitive side was kicking in, as it has throughout my journey.

I just walked by; not my business. I then asked the supervisor if he knew the guy who died. He said no, but he was the one who found him. I then mentioned the owner's cooking pills, which I found on the internet. He said, "I'd rather not talk about it, but you could be on to something." We had that discussion because a girl was working as a housekeeper there and heard us talking. She said that the owners let others from the area come in and make meth during the winter. She said she had to clean up their messes afterward.

I don't have proof, but her words matched the owner's repeated offenses. The girl went on to mention how the owners would take bags of cash back home with them in the summer, which is a sign of money laundering. Oh well, not my business. She was just straight-up telling me all this without me even asking...

As we went back down to the lobby (mind you, I'm two months into this job), a guy came in and delivered hats, shirts, and other items in boxes. The supervisor said that was the "manager's uncle." As the "Uncle" bent down, I saw a gun—a GUN!—in his back pocket, not in a holster. That tells me there are drugs in those boxes. Wouldn't that be your thought too? As he left (this was a test), the housekeeper asked if I saw the gun. She was there and saw it too.

I acknowledged that I saw the gun as the guy left. He had a yellow smiley face sticker on the driver's side back window. That indicated that if a trooper pulled him over, the uncle would have dispersed his weapon. The housekeeper, who had told us about it, threatened to stab me if I said anything and even pulled out her knife. I messaged the GM and the manager about it, but the GM had already left, and the manager wasn't there. Then the housekeeper went into the GM's office, shut the door, and I heard snorting again.

What I also thought was weird was that before we went up to do a check-around and the GM left, when I heard the GM say those things about the leak, he turned off the cameras and yelled, "Cameras need fixing." If you see the screen out, then this guy delivers boxes with drug products. I couldn't look because it was a felony. The next day, I got a call saying I was fired. A note was mailed with my last check, saying I was creating a hostile work environment. Nothing about the meth or pills was mentioned as the reason. It was because they knew I had seen the gun, and I had a feeling the housekeeper was behind it too. So, with all that has happened, the people who used to run it when I first worked there didn't have this going on. Now, I must find another job. AGAIN. They put their employee in a dangerous position. Walk away from your job if you ever see something like that.

During this time, I came across a Facebook page of someone who was a palm reader. One thing I didn't mention about my past is that when I was 12, I got my palm read, and she told me I would be "good with my hands." This current palm reader was able to describe what my old boss looked like—the one who was in NC at the marketing company. I couldn't keep my momentum together. I was anxious to know how! He explained, "When I was young, my parents put me in a psych ward." Later, his family understood what he could do—see the realms and interests of others.

He didn't use it to deceive others; he used it to help! So that's why I said, don't judge me just yet! Because if that's the case, we have a lot of judging to do on others! But I say no, why? After what I had learned, I took the information in like it was a new world. Don't be afraid to submerge yourself in different ideas. These differences will help us find answers. If you don't seek them, how would you know? If you don't know, how will you learn?

During this time, he asked, "Why did you go to the lady who did that to you?" Which made me realize he was for real unless he was part of her cult (who knows). Anyway, I told him, "She got ahold of me." When I complained about my roommate online, I went to her and told her my thoughts and a couple of other dreams. *I didn't mention it before because I knew it would eventually be addressed within this timeline of events.*

I told him I expressed to her that I felt like we were all getting hurt. I told him about a dream I had where people were getting tossed all over. It was meant to show chaos in society by ghost figures or ghosts of immigrants. Another dream I explained involved me hiding under a silver cloth, running away from a big bug, and then being on a boat, getting chased by people shooting guns. The palm reader said I would see that day very soon. I then told him about the day the news reported a shooting at a business in another state. I had a dream that conflicted with the shooting, and the building looked exactly like what I had seen on the news the day after my dream. The palm reader expressed his certainty and told me to come back again another time.

He was right! Dreams are sometimes a symbol of our path. The dream about the bug and the boat? Well, before I went back to the palm reader, the dream came to life. My parents had a roach issue because we live near the woods. They had to call the exterminator, and the guy came and gave us covers for our beds. Before he left, a movie was on, and in it, they were on a boat getting chased! **So, from the dream, it was me hiding from a big bug figure under a type of sheet cover and then running onto a boat getting chased.** The meaning? It proves you're on the right path when you see a dream play out.

I then rethought the water gun dream I had. There must be something there that allows us to see things in our dreams. What type of sorcery is this? So, I decided to follow a spiritual path. It allows you to be more open than being forbidden to try new things due to a corrupt religion. I say that because we learn what is taught in schools… Catholics took people and told them, "Don't do this. God will not save you," to put you on a leash! We aren't supposed to eat pigs, nor should some eat shellfish, nor should some shave their legs. This is something I didn't learn from the Bible but from our school's social studies book. The church did that to help communities prevent crime. Which, in a sense, isn't a dreadful thing.

That showed us how the suppression of our existence started. Back then, things were not as understood as they are now in our present days. The next day came around, and I saw the palm reader again. I expressed what I wanted to mention to him: one more thing about "Charmed," the show.

"If the Royals, & Vatican have records & books of Demonology & Witchcraft, maybe that too, should be a sign. Be of Good Light."

– Lyle

Our very existence relies on the Pope. When the Bible talks about evil existence, it is not just the fallen; it is the spirits. If you remember me talking about this, go back to Chapter 5 and review "Spirit." I then kept deliberating on my discussion with the palm reader.

Another part of the unknown? Yes, we have had hidden technology that you see today throughout the 2024 years of our existence on this Earth. The Pope has a book of "Bad Spirits," as they go around Spain. I told him I wanted to recap more about my sister. She had this friend from Spain who was adopted by her current adopted father, who was military. She said that when she was little, she came over to sleep at our house when I was young. My sister and she are the same age. She said, "I saw something hovering over you, protecting you."

Years later, as I kept expressing to the palm reader, we went to a bar, she and I, the girl from Spain, to catch up as family friends. There was this girl in the bar, and out of 50 others there, she looked at me and said, "I'm adopted." For some reason, I asked her, "Did someone pass away when you were adopted?" She was in disbelief. She said it was her brother in a car accident. I said, "It wasn't an accident." There was guilt. She said, "He did things to me, and he couldn't live with himself." She told me her parents went to mediums, and she did not believe them until I showed up and expressed what others had said.

That being said, the Pope DOES know what happens spiritually. Why do you think he is now addressing love for all? It is not a coincidence. We have matters in life that need only the strong to deliver the right prescription to defeat evil spirits. You can only defeat the wrong if you do not allow your mistakes to get in his way. Those who abuse you and pursue your mistakes? Go back while you are alive and fix them to repent for your sins. Because if you fix what you have broken, evil cannot use that against you.

"As Christians, Catholics & ALL others, need to come together. With a better understanding of our moral grounds. Not separate issues. Unity is key, why preach & don't commit?"

– Lyle

As I explained to the palm reader, he acknowledged the differences in the seven religions below before I finally left. "This is to give you a general idea of things," he noted, "not to mock or denounce one or make you follow one, only to offer a unique perspective, as most religions could learn from each other. Not to divide but to be equal to all. Not just for some."

Our higher power exists, or which God do you follow? There are over 4,000 religions across our world. These are just the top seven known belief systems. I do not want to study them all or mention a lot of information, just to give you vague ideas on what we are learning from.

ISLAM – (Isa – The God they name and the rest that follow below as is) – Old teachings are said, and current ideals of Islam are read wrong, as current Islam now endures violence toward those who don't believe in Allah. They also believe in an "eye for an eye"—what you do to others comes back to you. Some people throughout history, no matter the religion, believed that to be a good form of punishment.

HINDUISM – Ishu – also believes in reincarnation – views that the Universe is God, and everything in the Universe is God and seeks divine truth in all life forms.

JUDAISM – Yeshua – also believes in reincarnation – views that God is one and of no form and created the world. To God alone, may one offer prayer.

BUDDHISM – Buddhism is considered a philosophical approach to life more than a religion. Also believes in reincarnation – Follow gracious acts to receive abundance,

139

Christians and Catholics (Jesus Christ) do not support reincarnation or its meanings. These two follow the same aspects of the Bible teachings but have different approaches to certain scriptures. Go back to the New England Territory days of the 1290s, as the Christians did kick Jews out, just so you are aware of that. Some good Christians were also light workers, helping the throne of God. Keep in mind, around the 4th Century, early Christians used the term Paganism for those who practiced polytheism and not Judaism. Polytheists believed in more than one God. The Catholic Church wanted nothing to do with any of them; they had their own belief system. One I would particularly suggest following if you want more restrictions on your self-minded freedoms and no adaptability to changes in your environment due to self-enclosure. The spiritual self allows freedom of growth, as religion only allows circumference—a distance around a circle, which is enclosed, can only let you go so far before you are running around in your own hamster wheel. This is about perspectives—to show we should all come together, not war with each other! I am giving vague events that did happen for you to GET IT, supplied together. I have met more Christians today who support reincarnation. Hmm...

"I also foresee iRobots might be closer to our existence than ever before. These will help with future wars, particularly in very bad scenarios or possibly space. They will help create structures for the human race. Let's just hope not of a police state of controlism. Then, find weapons that can electrocute them in some fashion, maybe. This one is an LOL for me." – Author

Presbyterians—Follow what the apostle Paul taught: no one is good enough to deserve salvation. Thus, we are saved only by grace because God decided to save us through Jesus' incarnation, death, and resurrection.

When I left the palm reader, he told me to "be careful." I kept thinking... what did he mean by "be careful"? Was it that deceivers are afraid to come forth with sin? So they blame me? To hide their troubles?

I wanted to mention reincarnation in our reading because, with all I have been through, the "jolting" I felt on the porch at five years old? That's when I first got my "conscience." I felt like I came from a different world. I felt like I lived this life at another time also because it did seem like certain people knew me or wanted to drug me, so I would not inspire my true path.

The following day, I woke up with another message: The technology I mentioned before, that we have had since the beginning? It also allows us to travel to other planets that have our existence. These people are "hopefully better civilized." James Webb's telescope has found Earth-like planets, heartbeats, and other radio signals throughout our galaxy. We are not alone. AND do not dwell on what we cannot reach but on what we may carry out. In other words, our history is well hidden. Some cannot fathom the destruction of our past leaders, so we suppress ourselves from knowing. On this Earth, we must find meaning in our lives. That is why I am trying to deliberate with the uninformed! Not spreading disinformation, only to advise the not-so-wise!

"If we can't survive on a planet or terraform it, if such surface isn't suitable but ground is good, with the right outfits, you can create a silo/ greenhouse for entities below surface that holds 5,000-10,000+. Scattered & connected by others within."

-Lyle

Consciousness: my soul is my consciousness, or rather, my consciousness is my soul; they are one and the same. For my consciousness or my soul moves within me, guides me, and connects me to reality.

As the Spirit educates the believer's conscience about the things of God, the personal standard formed by the conscience begins to align with the standard of revealed truth.

The reason I mentioned reincarnation is because of my spirit. Everyone gets a chance to experience everyone's life. It is how your work reflects humanity that determines your next mission when you die and whether you repent to have the choice to move on, if done well enough, to explore other worlds. Or you can choose to be in the "Matrix" of reincarnation. The matrix of our life? It is when you step outside your mind to realize, again, that our laws are set in place to make you not question. When do you start to question things? It is when you realize the matrix is another way of "suppressing." Choose to see the world for its true self or stay in a basic format.

Those who have not foreseen the truths? I hope you understand again that I am not baptized or religious. I am just following what my path prevails me to do.

Those who see an entity standing on clouds and those who are in white cloaks are the Guardians/Elders of protection, protecting YOU (another vision, within this process I had). I wanted to share these aspects because those who know, understand, and believe. Those who do not? They have plenty of time to foresee the unseen. Remember when I mentioned asking to know about life as a kid? At an early age, our energy is stronger. You must be careful what you ask for. It is an old-time saying... words are powerful. So are our actions!

Now, the seven religions I vaguely described? If you are curious, you can now venture off and discover more ideals you wish to learn. (HOPEFULLY FOR THE GOOD) As I rambled on in my head, I figured... what if I talked to my parents about it? Ha. They did not want to hear anything I had to say about this. I started drinking more and smoking more (pot), which was very deep in my head. I was depressed and arguing more with my parents. I tried not to. They just did not make it easier on me. Knowing they were part of what happened. At least, that is what I think and feel. I started thinking I needed a therapist. Due to a lack of understanding from my parents, I wondered, *Are they not talking to me about it? Do they know I have the power of wisdom to find out myself without explaining?*

Well, my sister then came up and suggested I could come down and stay with her and her girlfriend. I figured, why not? She lives 2 hours away. So, here we go. Now, I am living with my sister and her girlfriend. I got myself settled with a therapist and a job at a college serving the students in the kitchen. It did not last long because of COVID. A fake vaccine to dispose of de-population. I jabbed myself with one of the vaccines at the pharmacy when it came out. I wish I had not. It has been shown that it changes DNA functions and can damage your genes. However, I have not had any issues with it so far. As I hope not. I say this because, again, you must question things before you make a split decision. I did not question it. Now? Several doctors are coming out against it.

So, are you going to listen to the ones trying to save us? Or deceive us? Throughout my stay, I stopped smoking and eating healthily, and my dreams became vivid. One I received was about how the glaciers were melting, and the government had these metal containers that were supposed to withstand the disaster. Everyone in my family was rushing to get on before it wiped us away. Then, it would switch to being in space, fighting through Space Force against others. * I would have a dream within a dream. *- As the meaning would be, the spiritual side is communicating double messages at the same time. Just an FYI... but before I woke up? The third thing I saw and remember was seeing cards in my hand with the numbers 3.6.9. *I would also see these three numbers on license plates, too, every day I was out driving. *

"If of any threats exist in Space as Space Force evolves, it could be from before, when the Fleets or old past Military/ Gods founded earth, (hell) after they civilized other areas before us, we would face the other realms of technologies if we were to come in contact."

– Lyle

These three numbers stand for a powerful message from the universe that your creative energies and spiritual growth are aligned, and it's time to focus on serving humanity and finding your purpose in life. Any guardian of yours will support your motives. – Throughout my path, when did I become ordained? I sat in my sister's living room, watching a Netflix show "Grace and Frankie." They had a scene where Frankie had to get ordained to officiate her ex-husband's new wedding. I felt pushed to become ordained. I then performed four weddings, stayed there, and did 3 Reiki trial treatments, with INCREDIBLY honest feedback. * If you want to do Reiki? I would suggest not going to classes if you can do it on your own. I am self-taught and was born with Reiki. When the lady who read my palms told me I was good with my palms? I have now found my meaning. But I do not willingly spread my energy. People love taking others' energy. Be careful. The ones who call themselves masters will use that title to go above you. You cannot "actually heal," but it is a pain-releasing substance through our energetic system. * Use wisely, my friend. Do not pay extreme prices for something you can be taught on your own. Guess what I did?

Your "right hand" is the positive battery, and the "left hand" is the negative battery. Once you put your hands up in a clapping position with both hands facing each other, waving them around in a ball, you can feel the different translucent waves. If you can, then I have taught you about yourself. It is not my job to give you all the answers but to supply facts and deliverance throughout my journeys. As you know, this is not about exhaling everything I have been through, but rather important parts, to provide the right presentations to the value of my attributions.

I was then watching a show called "Mom." It was the same day I signed up to do Reiki. The mother in the scene is played by Allison Janney. In this scene, she was thinking about drafting a book. Then it hit me—that "feeling." It struck me like when I saw the scene that inspired me to become ordained and practice Reiki. So that is why I am doing this! Let whatever spirit drive me to my destination.

As I hope to help you, certain evildoers will try to demolish our existence through spiritual warfare. Do not let them strip you of the heavenly gifts you can offer our world. For whatever it may be, maybe write your own journey down, let others see your experiences, and learn from the knowledge you can share. Nothing is impossible in what we can do. Do you think this was easy to write? Some things take time; for some, they come quickly.

It is only impossible if you are not looking in the right direction. As I say that... Is there anything in your life that you want to help people with? That you know you can do? If so, you may have found your purpose. It can be small or big. Anything helps. I delivered bags of food to random people and the police station anonymously. Why? Not for ego or the "seeking" of getting patted on the back. It is not what I strive for. Some people were able to receive a meal, and that is all I wanted to feel good about. I sleep better at night, knowing I have made up for mistakes or done honorable deeds. All paths are shaken at some point. Come to think of it, do dreadful things really happen to good people? Do we really know what they could have done behind "closed doors" to leave early? Or what we had done in our past lives? God takes those for a reason. A reason He must have...

As good prevails over wicked ways, I hope we learn this before the end days. Turn on our "light" and seek effective ways. Our hearts are the path to what we shall raise. We still have time to turn things around for the better. Don't you want to fight and keep God's praise?

– Lyle

One other revelation I need to share before we move on to the next chapter, and then I'll let you be. When COVID hit, seven months before it did, I wrote in a small book. I also expressed this to a lady I met at Walmart, who was named Dawn Stephenson. She is my witness and can attest to it. We all should stop working before our government makes us. I knew something bad would happen; I just didn't know the term. It was just for us to take control again. Due to the blind, I didn't speak up because who would hear my call to save us? So, I buried my notes on a hill inside a plastic bag not far away. I hope it's still there by that tree, though.

One voice can only speak so loudly to make the blind see. How much will it take before we suffer more? We, THE PEOPLE, shall not let any failed leadership remain in power that puts danger upon this land and its people of Sovereignty. They shall be stripped of their duties and rights as consequences are enacted by THE PEOPLE, said the spirit to the writer…

PLEASE DON'T GO.

"Nothing is impossible in what we can do, but it is only impossible if you're not looking or asking in the right direction."

– Lyle

Chapter 11: Getting Evidence

"Life isn't just finding a needle in a hay stack, sometimes? It's finding that 1 hay stack to reach your height of accomplishments through a world that pricks. Some people are just the needle."

- Lyle Light

I was just sitting around wondering about life in those days. A couple of months went by while I still worked. On one of my days off, I got a call from my boss, and she told me that they had to let me go. They paid me very well, and I was able to save $5000, and I had saved every penny from my Job. That was not bad at all.

My sister was looking for another car for me. She thought I was going to buy a car with no muffler on it. I wanted to save because I did not have a job anymore. I bought the car in the end because the guy selling it had Jesus signs and said he was of faith. He said that the check engine light would not turn on, but the car was fine. He lied; there was a lot more wrong with the car. That was $5,000 down the drain. The car quite literally blew up.

You can say that was my fault or my sister's, but a man of faith lied. May he be abhorred for deceiving others with financial Ponzi schemes. One must work for their wage or live on donations.

So now, I decided to leave them, as it was for nothing... down the drain. And they wonder why I have anger issues. Our actions are causing a domino effect on what we deliver to someone else's life. That is why they say, "Treat others the way you want to be treated." This is where Yin and Yang come in.

*You must balance happiness, keep your mind busy, make art, make, or do whatever you forget yourself in those negative head space moments. Balancing negatives? It is playing into your enemy. You need to play the same card to demolish their evil tactics. *

*In Chinese thought, there are two great opposite but complementary forces at work in the cosmos. **Yin is the female, cold, dark, passive power; yang stands for masculinity, light, and warmth**. Earth, rain, soft, evil, black, small, and even (numbers) are yin; heaven, sunshine, hard, good, white, large, and odd are yang.*

Sometimes – Family can be both a negative and a positive influence on you. You must read into what is not being said. Negatives can lead us down our path.

I got put through that exorcism; could they have warned me? Not slither someone into it? Because of those doors, I saw? Nailed? 2 things came through my mind. The basement was used for a lab of some sort of imprisonment. Sometimes, we have an A. Answer and a B. Answer. Within time? You can and will find out. I have not found out yet as I am not involved in that part of their crimes. You do not nail doors shut all over just for "Rats." I am writing this to make people aware; watch out for whose presence you allow nearby. We do not really know who our friends are. I am not using that example as an over-exaggeration remark. This is something I felt. Deep down, I am trying to think they were good people. When the ex-roommate insisted, they were not. Why?

Well, before I left my sister's to go back to my parents? I randomly added her on Facebook, and she wanted to call me. After what happened? She thought I would befriend her and or her husband again. So, I went ahead to ask her, "Why" did that happen? (I was recording her) she said a lot of drugs were involved, and she had a girl following her from house to house. I may have cussed her out. I did not mean to. Wouldn't you? After everyone considers you nuts but gets a revealed truth? On recording! She also said, "I saw some crap in the kitchen when she did that thing and went back upstairs."

So now, I was sitting on proof of her drugging me. Shows not ever to give up. If you have a valid reason and proof, you have every right to fight for your life. It's our free WILL. What now? Welp. I cannot do anything on an authority level, but they know about it. Why? After the phone call, she called 911 and got me to be placed in the hospital, saying I was going to harm myself. The officer told me, "You're a male; you need to be more masculine." In other words, move on.

I personally thought the police were involved in this rhetoric. But as I got into the hospital, I sat in this room all alone; then they put this other guy across from me. He put the bed up, and the nurse let him punch it to leave out steam. I lay there for almost 2hrs. I said, "Is someone coming."

The nurse then came in and asked me what had happened. She legit said these words "She used Black Magic." You need to stay away from them, she insisted. She noted: "You are too sane to be here; nothing is wrong with you." I mean, I quit my therapist because she could not give me answers about what was happening to me. It is just someone complaining about your problems so they can "Prescribe" a drug someone is making a commission on. I just wish I could do something legally. NY had similar Witchcraft cases, due to NY making all this legal under law. So, should we make changes to these laws? It is legal for beneficial corrective use, but no restrictions. Though murder is illegal for all to commit, it is the ones hiding it that are the problem. Those who learn from the mistakes of others can manipulate the equilibrium to achieve their desired outcomes, balancing their actions to avoid getting caught.

Ralph and Mary Hall of Setauket VS NY State 1965 were accused of witchcraft and causing the death of their neighbor, George Wood, along with his child. At the time, New York law did not recognize witchcraft as a crime, so the case was prosecuted as a murder case.* Hmm…

So, were they trying to prep me? To take me to the basement? For a ritual? That is why it is always important to restrict certain people from knowing your abilities. They will consume you in ways you could not imagine. *My roommate explained there was this girl they used to hang out with who disappeared before I came into the picture.* After I heard that? I put my intuition to use and pieced it all together: these people killed her with all the information and tactics used against me. I was next. Or did they keep her as a prisoner?

I admire the power of my spirit and guardian to send me an answer - Cults run societies. Some are for good. The evil? They are hidden but in plain sight. Again, when are you open? Be careful where you do so. I wish I could provide more to stand for my conclusions on the lost girl. After everything, I know she got murdered. It is something you feel, know, and foresee from spirit. To the girl? I am sorry that it happened to you. May God rest your soul, and may you not suffer. The only reason I also say this? One time, before this all went down, I was exposed to voodoo. The mother asked if I could help clean her kitchen. I went ahead to do so, as she finished cleaning her fridge out. Then, she asked if I would clean her freezer for her. As I type this, look in my freezer; you, the reader, look in yours. There was blood scattered throughout, like meat was being put in the freezer uncovered. Was I cleaning up this missing girl's blood? This is when I realized I was being prepped. My fridge looks clean, as I am sure yours is not all bloody either. This was not just little; this was a lot. She asked me to use bleach! I did not say anything to her, due to not knowing the outcome. You know?

I think some will say I may be overthrowing unrealistic ideals. If only that was so…Also, Some parts of evil can be hidden by an invisible force that spreads to each person hate, disbelief, and division. It is our own job, once we gather that truth, to know how to protect ourselves...

So, what now? I went home after the hospital visit. I was talking to the older lady who was on the scooter at Pal-Mart. And what did she say after I expressed to her what happened? "What goes around comes around."

*If you are wondering about my dog? * - she is doing great and is healthy. She has kept me sane throughout my journey. I love her so much. Be dear to animals... speaking of dogs. I headed to this store near the house and I wanted to get treats for my dog and snacks for me, and for some reason. I really enjoy Sodas. Before I went further, I met this lady and dog. I want to add something here. *Our country is one of the ones that put cancerous chemicals in our food, so we again... supply more money to the pill industry. Noticed anything? How are pill industries, in fact, the only operation to legally smuggle opioids? The Clints who were running as President... They sold stocks in 2008, including Oil Companies & Pharmaceutical Companies, before having to take a position. They didn't want to cause a conflict of interest, but they complained to us about how prices were too high, but they didn't complain about that extra cash flow, did they? While you were hurting. Try doing it on the street for what they do and see where that gets you. Lol. Just something more to think about. We all know it is true.*

Also, if a leader or ex leader sends money overseas, and that same country's leader receives it and they turn up into your country after it was sent? That's a sign of money laundering. Only the bright, will see. As the dim are poisoned by the wizards. Like, Wizard of Oz and the yellow brick road, your told it's for good, but once you follow the road, you realize you were deceived and the reality was faked. We would be of similar times due to bureaucrat controlism, and the way you think. To get away with crimes against our tax dollars.

Sugar is an addictive drug, just as much as tobacco, weed, or other choices. Everything is a drug. So, guess what? Kids are receiving sugar. Are you getting drugged with sugar? Why do you think your kid yells when they don't get their fix of sugar? Or why do they throw tantrums when you do not buy them a treat at a store? *(I did that as a kid, when I was younger so I can relate, can you?)* Our body needs RICH raw vegetable and fruit diets. We are not made to dispose of processed food. Hence, gut issues, ulcers, or Diverticulitis are common. Do not eat seeds or peanuts in that condition. The body cannot digest hard food items. (Most will disagree) Eat and find out!!

The day before I met the lady, I was diagnosed with Diverticulitis, the same as my grandmother, father, and sister. It is inflammation in the digestive tract that causes pouches and hard foods to stay inside and collect as undigested food. *

Sorry, I did not mean to ramble on again. Can you forgive me? Anywho. While I was leaving the store, I saw this lady start walking with a dog. Guess what? Remember when I talked about my grandmother's Disney dogs in the photo I have? That's exactly the dog she had. Coincidence? Was this a sign that I needed to foresee the result? I stopped and asked if she wanted a ride. "Sure," she said. She only had to go back to the town I passed headed back to my parents. Our conversation felt like a lifetime. She was walking because she was visiting her sister. Her sister's husband was starting an argument about how she was not doing well enough and how he needed to work more to pay for bills and things. She told me her sister lost her job due to COVID-19. Is that her fault? She noted she was yelling back at him to calm down and rationalize himself. She told me he came after her, but her sister stepped in.

So, she took her dog and came out for a walk to buy cigarettes. She was stressed. Her dog was so cute. I then expressed to her, "You'll be okay," *and we started talking about similar aspects of life I talked about within this book- Then*, she talked about her kids and why they do not talk to her. They are upset that she left their father. She told me he was abusive, would drag her around the house by her hair, etc. I could not withhold a tear and expressed, "I'm sorry," my dad tossed my mom off the steps when I was a kid." I also noted, "I see your daughter coming to you soon, within a month. Your son is stubborn, and he, for some reason, does not agree with you more than your daughter." I said that to her without knowing which kid liked her the most. She told me I was right. We stayed connected, and she told me her daughter did eventually get ahold of her. It was about a month and a half after we met; I was close!

I did some more searching within this time to describe the evidence of what I learned about insinuating my adeptness. Do you remember me being in the bar showing the girl her revelations on how she disbelieved till I gave her insight on her - brother? *
Empath- An empath is a person highly attuned to the feelings and emotions of those around them. Empaths feel what another person is feeling at a deep emotional level. Their ability to discern what others are feeling goes beyond empathy, which is defined simply as the ability to understand the feelings of others. *

As days went by, one of my older cousins came around. He was living in Florida. His mom was my favorite aunt who had passed away. As mentioned in the beginning, she was kind to me. I said, "what're you doing back."

"Moving back." He said. He also had a baby and a wife. It did not take long to know they argued all the time. We had a drinking night with them and their friends.

I noticed that drinking can open our system more because it allows us to be relaxed. The only time the spirit turns on is not when stressed. Stress results in anger, and anger results in bad compulsions. Compulsions lead to consequences.

There was one friend who showed up with her boyfriend and started talking about how she had lost her kids, and her dad took care of them. Without saying anything about them, I was able to tell her that the "Older daughter is protecting the younger brother, as she knows the middle sister can help herself and the young does not pick up things as quickly. Your dad will come around; he is upset with you; he thinks he lost his daughter. He was once into drugs, but it feels like he failed you. He is angry at himself. He sees his past in you."

She explained, "He and I had this conversation just last week and couldn't believe you said that."

She replied, "You must be an empath."

We all had a good night afterward. Then, the next day, I continued to now look for another job again... guess where? Back at another job I used to work at - Stones Anchor Hotel. The one that had the flooding, and I did all the work and all? I thought of it because I saw an ad they were hiring online. So, I reapplied and finally got a supervisor position. The only exciting thing about being a Front Desk Supervisor? I got free meals and was able to use the "Security Walk Around," to not be at a desk full of insensitive employees. "Why" say that? I will explain that when I got hired, the manager did not tell the other supervisor I got hired as the 2nd supervisor. So, the 1st FDS thought I was taking her job. Now, she was in her mid-30s, as I was like 26. Yes, she was living with her parents, and so was I. But get this? *I figured out why she was in her place as she was. How? She told me...*

When I worked the first shift with her, getting to know her etc. She told me she "lost" her kids because she got into drugs and the wrong people. (There must be a lot of people out here getting involved in this messy substance, I say to myself.) I try to listen. Then we did a walk around. She told me how she was a sex addict, and she touched me on my shoulder. I had gone ahead to get my phone out and record her. (Sometimes, you must protect your well-being).

She would talk to me inappropriately very often. I then told my boss, as policy says, to go through the level of command. Mind you, most of the workers there liked me. I worked there for three months, and throughout that time, she kept talking to me about sex, trying to get me to have a conversation with her about it. She did this so that he could accuse me of starting the bad-mouth discussions. As time went by, a new woman got hired, and long story short... I had to get a recording of her stating... "I got hired to try to get you fired; you're a good guy." She then quit... within two weeks of being there!

I went to my manager about it. She did not know what to do! (Fire her so she stops the hostile work environment? Nope.) So, one night, I was working with the 1st FDS, who was the problem. She started talking about this one job she worked at - a pizza shop. In the beginning? I mentioned a job, personal assistant, remember? I do it in this way of deliverance, so I can keep you pondering to read my offerings. **

She told me the name of the business, "Jessie's Pizza Joint."

I told her, "No way! I worked there for five days."

She then expressed, "Why?"

I said, "When I got hired as the personal assistant, she would have me go to the bank for her, get food supplies at the store, organize advertisements to be mailed out, shop for her shopping list, and babysit her kid. She asked me to do a pizza run, you know, to go "deliver." She just started delivering the week I got hired. I came back from getting her kids from school. She handed me the food. She then told me to deliver something in this bag to a well-known customer who she knows. She said to "not look at it" because it was just something she owed him. (Ok? Goes through my mind) I looked... she was delivering weed and what looked like a white pill. After I got back. I told the boss, "I quit," As my boss used me to pawn her illegal sales!"

The coworker who was the other supervisor said when she worked there, a girl came in; the problem girl noted she felt like she was undercover trying to get information on the owner. As she said, "She is a busted drug dealer." And the authorities were after her. (I THEN thought she was the girl that was undercover.) *The demeanor of the way she delivered her statement made me question if it could be her.* One of the guys in the kitchen was there, and he noted the front desk would make a good "deal spot for drugs."

As the night proceeds, these kids came in off the street who were locals, and they were not allowed in the hotel because they wanted to use the pool. I told them no, go home. As I was going to do a walk around. The 1st FDS told the kids to hold on, and I was halfway down the hallway and tried to "Act" as I walked around the corner. But I did not. I saw her open the pool door for them. So, I kick them out! If something happened? She then blamed me because I was the MOD on duty at the time. She was not. She broke protocol! Then, it was time for us to go; the night audit came in. I must have one of them finish a sexual harassment course. She went above my say and told him, "Just sign it." She took it from my hands, he signed it, and she delivered it to the GM's mailbox.

She just went against Labor Law Violations!!!! This was very crucial and so arrogant. I was just trying to do my job at all these places.

And what did I get? Being told I am jealous of co-workers when I put 100% into my work! So, I wrote up an email because my hiring manager was not doing anything... So, I put the General Manager in the email, too, before I left. As I walked out, the guy from the kitchen and the 1st FDS were talking... I then heard the guy from the kitchen calling me "weird" and how they wanted to find a way to sell his drugs but did not want me up there. The next day, I woke up, and I looked at my work emails from my phone. My hiring manager told me, "I'm just throwing my colleagues under the bus." She was so unhinged that she was pitying herself for her own failed leadership. She thought that she could hide her wrongdoing by guilting me. I just thought, okay let the games begin.

I sealed the proof from all the people who tried to ruin me. It is the most comprehensible thing anyone can do to secure their spiritual path. The day ended with me knowing in my gut that I was telling the truth, but I also knew that I was going to be jobless once again. My gut told me that before I walked into my place of work again, I had to put my phone on record.

So, I did just that. I walked in, and my hiring manager asked me to go into her office. I did. She then told me I was getting a write-up, as I "apparently" could not make the team work together. She told me that I abused my privileges and thought it was about me… *I do not agree with violence, but I was fuming and really wished these people would dispose of themselves off this earth.* I continued to acknowledge I had a recording. She told me, "The only fool in this room is you."

She told me to go back to work. I said that I would, but first, I wanted to speak to HR. I told her everything; then, my hiring manager asked me to leave. Abusing her position, creating a hostile work environment, and violating basic civil working rights, she made me leave despite her knowing that I got sexually harassed. I kept asking to see the GM, but she was not there at the time. Her husband was because he was the "Head of Maintenance." The unintelligent HR lady went ahead to asked the GM's husband to escort me out of the building. I left my keys on the desk. As I turned around, I grabbed them. Guess what he did? He contracted his hand on the back of my neck, pushing me, resulting in him assaulting me. So, I will just skip ahead to let you know I AM NO FOOL. I reported them to the Division of Workers Rights, with my proof of sexual harassment, hostile work environment, and getting assaulted. As the DWR conducted their findings, they did find probable cause of the abuse. The best part is? The hotel sent the proof for me to them. The video recording showed the GM's husband assaulting me. As I read reports, they asked the Dept. of Labor Rights if I had proof of turning them in. Guess what the DOLR said? "Yes." Not only did they lie. They lied in the report, saying the GM and her husband, Head of Maintenance, were in the room when she gave the write-up and when she told me to leave. As my recordings SHOWED they lied everywhere as they thought they could ruin me. I listened to the Spirit... As it protected me.

The current findings are fines against the establishment and a prolonged battle ahead in court. Right now? I am taking time to enjoy life. I am living basically. It is okay not to have a new phone, a new game console, a new car, or a new iPad or laptop. It is okay to not give corporations any more of your money. It is okay to not eat three times a day, as I eat twice a day. I have seen myself lose weight easier and feel better. I found a good, mindful place after all the abuse of others, as I did not let them destroy me, as they made me stronger. Now that I'm dealing with Court findings, I found 2 jobs while waiting for the verdicts.

I am working seasonally at a local Mom and Pop Wine and Beer company called "Wolf Den IPA and Wines." FYI, I do not drink IPA. Some of you know what hairspray tastes like when you spray it, and it has a strong alcohol smell. Yep. Hairspray = IPA. You drinkers judge me! I do not care. Anywho, I like mom-and-pop places.

Places that are not corporations supply history, knowledge, and experience through arduous work and allow you to be yourself. Corporations supply knowledge and some history, but they will easily replace you. They do not let you be YOURSELF.

THANK YOU to the people who hired me for this seasonal job. You know how to treat people and give support when needed. Your family business is a definition of respect for its community. You cannot compete with employers who treat their employees well. Hopefully, I am good enough to add to that establishment. Thank you for giving me a shot. You know who you are! I like sweet/semi-sweet wines. Occasional dry ones... The dryer, the healthier, from what I've been told.

One more revelation I need to add. The Mom and Pop Company position is just a fill-in seasonal for when they need me. Do you remember when I mentioned staying with my sister and her girlfriend, eating healthy and meditating more? I had another "Sight" when I was leaving them to go back to NY, where I would be in an Automotive business setting. I am now working at Buyer Auto as the Assistant Manager. The dream also enclosed three people like the show "Charmed," the power of the 3, as I would make the 4th team member of this small auto family. They didn't see my mistakes on record as not being able to get hired but saw how my skills and experiences were conditioned to fit Buyer Auto. These "sights" are one of the reasons why I wrote this. I did explain to my ex-friend/roommate's boyfriend before I left them that I saw myself working in the Auto Industry. Plus! The dream at my sisters I mentioned? Could that have been another premonition?

As this is the second job I found prior to the mom-and-pop IPA, the dealership ended up being corrupt. The guy who hired me, being a local legislator, put $900 bills in a $1000 wrapper to blame someone else. Then I found out his bff assistant has a black book about his mistakes, and she told me as well that he also let someone buy a car, leaving the previous person's name on all the paperwork; they could have lost their license as his asst. secretly sent info about it to the main office. He has a % in the company, so he does as he pleases. So I dipped after 4 months as I found out his daughter is also a sheriff. Does he use the system to protect his image? I think yes, so why be around that? I help the mom-and-pop place once in a while now, as I'm staying low! No matter where I work, I'm a magnet to corruption, and I'm here to help stop it as it finds me. Is that why I'm here and a part of my purpose's path?

If you are a butt kisser? You are the sheep. Do not be a sheep! I have learned to forgive my parents as well. I know you were wondering about that. Again, you can forgive and not forget. Some? They do not need to be in your circle, though. I do forgive my sister as well. Since I found out she and her girlfriend are getting married at some point, I would love to officiate it. Or even sing a song for them too. Who knows if I don't? I will not get mad. I have just allowed SPIRIT to guide me to the right areas I need to be in. Paths might be shaken, yours too, but I will preach that everything happens for a reason. Yeah, I have cussed some people out in my time and showed some anger, but I have fixed a good part of my mistakes. As the Holy Bible said, "Behold I am coming as a thief, Blessed is he who watches and keeps his garments, lest he walk naked and they see his shame." -Revelation 16:15

Is it metaphorically speaking for our time? Your electronic devices are a "trap" to gather everyone's right or wrongs for data, which is the new gold. I do not want your things; I just want us to share, be happy, and stop causing destruction for our own good.

"I think the people who have experienced the most sadness are the ones who are always trying to make other people happy. Because they know firsthand what it's like to feel empty and depressed, and they don't want anyone else to feel that way."

– Robin Williams

The Holy Bible also noted, "He who is unjust, let him be unjust still; he who is filthy, let him be filthy still; he who is righteous, let him be righteous still; he who is holy, let him be holy still." – Revelation 22:12 If they are not hurting you, causing pain, physically, mentally or stealing, leave them alone! Leave the judging to our higher powers. We judge corruption, murderers, rapists, unethical destructive humans against their own.

As I sit back to enjoy this aspirational journey of waiting for the litigation of known facts, knowing my path is now starting to blossom to its purpose of both verdicts on my old ex-friend/roommate drugging me, her friends exorcism on me and the one against the hotel, of recorded evidence of them both lying, which leads me to conspire karma putting those into a mental home and financial losses to my gain as I have had the opportunity of privilege, through the spirit of protection, to weed out the unintelligent individuals who deceive their own denials. I spend my time with family, my beautiful beagle, and the very few friends I have. For those struggling through different or similar paths? This is for you <3 Own your ground, find your truth, do not complain if you do not have tenacity or valuable information, and organize your corrective responses. Do not ever be feared; knowledge is power, but learn from others! Frederick Douglass once said, "Knowledge Unfits a Man to be a Slave."

Remember- Rough drafts of your path. Would it be the only way to start finalizing your imperfections? Then, grow yourself into perfection.

Solidarity is how we win in Unity. Keep in mind that I did not graduate and I authored this book. All you need to do is find YOUR light! I found mine, and so can you! Find it, and do not let anyone dim you down. If a flower does not bloom, are you going to check the soil and the environment to find the root issue, or toss it out and blame the flower?

If you find yourself alone, note that its easier than keeping up with the circus of fools.

"Your loneliness is often the consequence of being authentic and true to yourself. Instead of being surrounded by fools who don't understand you, I'll sign up for that in any life."

–Author

"Those wondering why every generation is either good or bad? It's due to racism, being passed down generationally, why follow hate of your ancestors, they didn't know better as much as some still don't today."

– Lyle Light

"Life isn't just finding a needle in a hay stack, sometimes? It's finding that 1 hay stack to reach your height of accomplishments through a world that pricks. Some people are just the needle."

–LyleLight

"You're gonna be called crazy. They called Noah crazy, but when the flood came. All the fact checkers died." - Senator John Neely Kennedy

- Lyle Light

Most religions are set up in this one factor.

Suppress is Religion. If Jesus was spiritual? Then Free Will is what God gave us, as that's the Christianity Message. Judge actions, not love. That's it."

– Lyle Light

Genesis 2:15: God created humans to work

Ephesians 4:28: Paul encourages the idle to work with their hands to help those in need.

Be within your mind & heart to find your Golden S. Not your ego.

You May Go Now – God's Son

You may be lied to, talked about, or plotted against and still win with God.

To the lady who came in at my job, the mom-and-pop place. Thank you for not saying anything about me or my struggles. This made my day. Thank you, Amber! I will always keep the $2 bill, in reminder of you. She wrote - "May all of your enemies have flaky skin." How sweet!

If anyone who still judges/conflicts with this narrative of coming together, stopping hate, and just simply being miserable and still blaming others? Then, you cannot be saved if you still deny it. If you have made it this far, then you have given yourself the ability to be a human being. We are all out here trying to do our best. Anyone does not know anything more than others. Everyone in this world has lied about something or taken something from someone and tried to hide their own mistakes. If you have the time, you have the choice to make up for what you need to do.

Will we use our mistakes to better ourselves. Good prevails over the Evils. I am not pressuring anyone to follow any religion, nor am I asking you to meditate. I am just simply explaining my path of occurrences, what I've learned, and passing something on to help another hurting individual so that they now know there is Hope! If you follow Faith, then comes Clarity! YOU do not have to believe me, but examine my story and seek answers in your heart. Thank you for listening and passing me along or keeping this book. Remember - You can author your story too! Also, you must go through hoops sometimes to get where you need to be!

To the Involved- I'm not sharing my path to save myself from anyone's negative opinions of me. I don't care what happens to me or what is said about me. I've paid my dues and gone through my fair share of hurts and losses. This is my Revelation of God who saved me. He wants this story for us all to see; we need to learn to live in the now and learn what we're doing to each other. The ones involved know who you are. Reflect on yourself before you desire harm. I'm sorry to those who think I wish harm on you or a family member. That is not so. We say things when we're angry. Kids will go through their parent's "Cycle of Life." They will experience similar journeys to yourself, including pain. Through this journey, God wants you and ALL of us to apologize. Break the cycle of curses. Say, "I'm sorry." I am not baptized or religious. God and I found each other unexpectedly. You can find him too.

I just hope I help someone, maybe in getting out of their cultural atrocities that they think are hard for them to escape. Share the story you were born to tell if you are a Savior Survivor yourselves like I am. Don't be scared. I was for a while, but I realized they could not hurt me. Being afraid only drains your energy to the point of getting a lower vibration, it leads to depression and then to suicide. That's the energy vampire. Beware and take control! Namaste. We're better than this… All the real monsters in this world are humans, need to save ourselves from ourselves…

7 things the Higher Power dislikes – 1. A lying tongue

2. A proud look

3. Hands that kill innocent people

4. A mind that works up evil plans

5. Feet that are quick to do evil

6. A witness who lies

7. Someone who starts arguments among families

"The ones that came here 2024 years ago were God & Mary as Mary gave birth to Jesus when they founded Earth. As they were also Giants. 1st and 2nd awakening was when Earth was founded to keep civilization going & the birth of Jesus when they arrived. We are now in 3rd awakening. If gods are considered all dead? Who will save us now?"

- Lyle

Here's a song lyric I came up with for you, the reader. Thank you for reading me. I hope this helps you more.

"Life was tough, felt like a lonely fight,

Friends turned fake, only shadow in the night.

I stumbled, faced rejection, the pain ran deep,

But found my strength, while climbing from the steep.

In the silence I heard, a whisper so clear,

God's love surrounded, wiping away my fear.

[Chorus]

I found my power, rising from the ground,

No more doubt, now my voice is loud.

Rejection can't break me, I'm standing tall,

With faith as my guide, I'll conquer it all.

[Verse 2]

Growing stronger, with every single tear,

Learned to trust myself, let go of the sneer.

Now I walk with purpose, light ignites my way,

Embracing who I am, every step I sway.

Faith's my armor, I'm ready for the storm,

With God beside me, I'll always feel warm.

[Chorus]

I found my power, rising from the ground,

No more doubt, now my voice is loud.

Rejection can't break me, I'm standing tall,

With faith as my guide, I'll conquer it all.

[Outro]

So here I go, embracing the new,

With love in my heart, I know what is true."

– Lyle

"Be a free thinker, and don't accept everything you hear as truth.
Be critical & evaluate everything you believe in."

- Aristotle

I want to talk about String Theory for a quick moment & Space craft. I think I may be right. I don't want to get into all the math or all crucial parts. String theory is a physics concept that proposes that the fundamental building blocks of the universe are not point-like particles, but tiny, vibrating "strings" through which, depending on how they vibrate, manifest as different particles like electrons and photons, essentially creating all matter and forces through their various vibrational states. They're trying to figure out how to verify the predictions. How? It's invincible. To find the charge of protons, neutrons, and electrons, remember that protons have a positive charge (+1), neutrons have no charge (0), and electrons have a negative charge (-1); meaning the charge of an atom is calculated by subtracting the number of electrons from the number of protons.

It's an Invisible force of connective energy that's full of positive & negative. It's like batteries stacked like one another but negative down, positive up, and 0's swings out. Similar to leafs on a tree branch, it is connected to a stem of energy that's tiny and strong and has wave lengths that are a constant on going force as the particles are within the wave lengths. Think of it as looking up at a bright blue sky, that if you see small squiggly clear lines. Will be the energy you see. When you look at the sky, you primarily see light energy which is a form of electromagnetic radiation, specifically visible light, coming from the sun and other celestial bodies like stars and the moon; this is the only type of energy that the human eye can directly perceive. Unlike protons, neutrons and electrons as these are similar but invincible.

1.

1×7

2. 0. 0. 3.

-1×7   .

4.

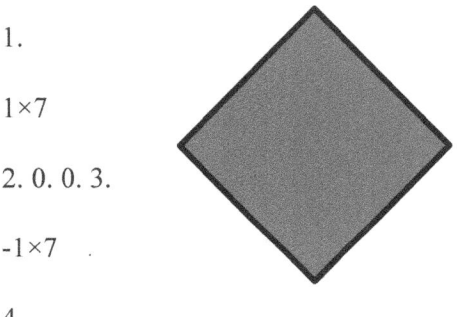

The sharp edges are worm holes that boost travel.

1×0−7×−1+7÷7×4= 11 dimensions of gravity travel paths. Assuming many more throughout the galaxy.

Similar to a diamonds structure. Again, the edges are worm hole like. As we're at the top, the lowered gravity forces are below and scattered around us but aligned magnetically invincible. Gravity is natural rather than a force. Similar to Terrance Howard's claims. If we were to use it as time travel, you would need to understand gravitational energy that works with spacecraft through wormholes. Such as creating a magnetically drivable fleet/ship with the Crystal Hematite & Black Tourmaline to support negative charge with high protection against high heat temps, & Diamonds, Ruby's to Sapphire, that will protect positive energy and heat temperatures. With small parts of clear quartz & using Photonic Crystals on the outer layer of craft that's used to cool solar panels. We use it for ours we use now for homes, businesses etc. You would also apply solar panels on such space craft for energy.

The element most commonly associated with both strong magnetic properties and high heat resistance is cobalt; particularly when used in alloys like "Alnico" (aluminum, nickel, and cobalt), which are considered ideal for high-temperature magnetic applications. This is also used in motors, & some sensors for vehicles, etc. Anything using a motor (Typically). This would be used as a motor with the sensors & apart of the magnetic structures.

As Below the craft & sides would result in magnetic force added with this such element. As if you were stuck you'd float in space not drop. So magnetically speaking, you should travel with the right elements added to the spacecraft. That's if gravity is natural in space, not a force, like we observe. You should travel easily. AI will also be a beneficial opportunity for this method, as it would be installed into all fleets & offers solutions to complex systems needing development.

Nuclear energy is already being used in some spacecraft, primarily in the form of radioisotope power sources (like RTGs), and there are active plans to develop and utilize nuclear thermal propulsion systems for future missions, potentially enabling faster and more efficient travel to distant destinations to planets. Making nuclear energy a significant part of future spacecraft power sources. So applying them with the certain stones/crystals. You might have found a way of travel.

Again, solar energy will be highly beneficial with spacecraft needing another Stone/Crystal- (Crystalline Silicon) is used in solar panels to convert light into electricity, but it can also be used to help cool solar panels. They also need this for what we currently use. I am sure there is more too it, but you never know. As the solar will help keep the craft going with electricity. That's why there's Suns, throughout our Galaxies.

Another form of a craft would insist of the solar, and crystals to cool the craft, as the underline spectrum would be designed for a similar affect of Searl Affect Generator that spins around in circle like a multiple magnetic system that spins off a magnetic application type of force with positive and negative charges against each other, acting like a spark of to transform and transfer the friction of energy produced is the main function of a UFO as it supplies faster travel, and the beings inside won't feel it spin, as the part the spins is a outer layer to the layer that sustains gravity within the craft. The more you know.

I also conclude that we might be in the middle of the diamond shaped (idea) as it's invisible, if the right craft, at the right point, will be gravitational or a leap at the outer part of the diamond structure (light- speed) as if we are light in space, then something light, can go light speed. As If space is light, anything of space will be light, due to gravity being a natural rather than a force, like on earth. So, anything will travel of light speed.

Food for thought.

Lyle Light

"If you question me, I'd admire you to question Royals, Popes & our standards of lies, as it's said, people like me are doomed, but only because they don't want it to change for the better, to deceive us, as should they question themselves."

– Lyle

"After the Big Bang, as if we came from other places, it was with the Animals we see with their DNA carried on the fleets & created different species. The Alien was created by the organism that grew from the (Eve) Energy and (Adam) Atom, with space particles that labored them. That Alien God, then used DNA structures to invoke the human species as only certain species can survive in certain atmospheres. Jesus and God then would be of a different human look. As most humans would be terrified of his look and expect him to be of Evil, because Humans judge base off looks thereof. That's why I say he isn't white. Think of him as scales/smooth skin on the body and with black eyes or with a tear drop eyes & tall. As if maybe our God, is the ET alien Area 51 uses to receive tax money from, then say you must be one of those tin foil hat guys to believe it. As I follow the rope that leads me to the knots that make me understand the ties between our history. Then why did I crack our glass ceiling of existence? Or call me a tinfoil. While you still assume.

This is the best answer I can find upon my journey & shown of how we were created. How an idea used can be used, that brings us to a different outlook to the battles of our past & the now to concept thy truth we all seek."

– Author

"If people think your crazy, it's when you become wiser and more informed. Not due to your craziness, but to their illusion, as YOU threaten it."

– Author

"The truth can be divisive"

- Lyle Light

www.ingramcontent.com/pod-product-compliance
Lightning Source LLC
Chambersburg PA
CBHW041627140626
46547CB00031B/1104